Board games round the world

A resource book for mathematical investigations

Robbie Bell and **Michael Cornelius**

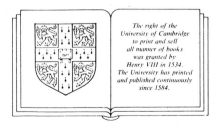

The right of the
University of Cambridge
to print and sell
all manner of books
was granted by
Henry VIII in 1534.
The University has printed
and published continuously
since 1584.

CAMBRIDGE UNIVERSITY PRESS

Cambridge
New York   Port Chester
Melbourne   Sydney

The authors

Robbie Bell is a retired consultant plastic surgeon and has written many books on the history of board games and also on eighteenth- and nineteenth-century tradesmen's tokens and Tyneside pottery.

Michael Cornelius taught in schools in Hertfordshire, Merseyside and Somerset before moving to the University of Durham where he is Senior Lecturer in Mathematical Education.

Acknowledgements

Many teachers and pupils have cooperated in work on the games described in this book. Particular thanks are due to staff and pupils in the following schools:

Durham School
Durham Johnston Comprehensive School
St Leonard's Comprehensive School, Durham
Park View Comprehensive School, Chester-le-Street

The photographs were taken by Robbie Bell and Ray Kitching.

Published by the Press Syndicate of the University of Cambridge
The Pitt Building, Trumpington Street, Cambridge CB2 1RP
40 West 20th Street, New York, NY 10011, USA
10 Stamford Road, Oakleigh, Melbourne 3166, Australia

© Cambridge University Press 1988

First published 1988
Reprinted 1990

Printed in Great Britain by Scotprint, Musselburgh, Scotland

British Library cataloguing in publication data
Bell, Robbie
  Board games round the world: a resource
  book for mathematical investigations.
  1. Mathematics – Study and teaching
  2. Board games 3. Educational games
  I. Title II. Cornelius, Michael
  510′.7′8   QA19.G3
  ISBN 0 521 35924 4   TSL

Contents

1 · Introduction: games and investigations

Board games have a universal appeal. There can be few people who have not, at some time, been excited or stimulated by a game. We enjoy leading an army to victory after outwitting an opponent, winning a race after devising a cunning and careful strategy, or defeating an adversary by skilful tactical play in a game of position. Equally the challenge of a 'solitaire' game where we pit our wits against the game rather than an opponent appeals to many. The history of games goes back many thousands of years and covers nearly all parts of the world. Some games depend on chance, some involve pure skill and strategy. The history of board games provides fascinating glimpses of life at particular times and in particular countries or continents – thus, for example, the twentieth century has produced 'race to the moon' games in America whilst the Egyptians some 4000 years earlier invented a race game with lions as pieces (*Senat*).

This book offers a *selection* of games chosen with both interest and possibilities for analysis and investigation in mind. The games are divided into five groups:

> Games of position
> Mancala games
> War games
> Race games
> Dice, calculation and other games

It is easy to invent headings but not always easy to classify, and hence some games could appear in more than one section. The best-known examples of games of position, war games, and race games are probably *Noughts and Crosses*, *Chess*, and *Backgammon* respectively. In any game of position it should be possible (but is not always easy!) to analyse strategies and decide on 'best' moves; likewise in war games such as *Chess* endless analysis can be carried out. Most race games on the other hand involve some element of chance (e.g. use of a die), but this does not preclude some thought being given to tactics in a game like *Backgammon* – only a very simple, straightforward race game, e.g. *Snakes and Ladders*, is a matter of pure luck for the players.

In trying to decide how best to play a particular game a player is forced into the need for logical thinking and thence, normally, to some mathematical thinking. For the games described in this book an attempt has been made to produce situations where some mathematical investigation can take place. Thus it is hoped that the ideas and suggestions may be of particular use to teachers in schools who are anxious to find material for pupil investigations or project work. A game may well provide motivation and interest as a starting point, and in some instances might lead to wider investigations in other areas (e.g. history or geography). It is important to bear in mind that games can be investigated at *many different levels* – among the suggestions made in the following chapters are some at a level which may be appropriate for a ten-year-old pupil (or younger) whilst others may be more suitable for an eighteen-year-old. Often it takes only a small modification to change an 'easy' task into a 'hard' one or vice versa, and both primary and secondary teachers will, we hope, find ideas which they can use. More importantly, teachers (and pupils) should find material here which will provide a stimulus for many other explorations beyond, and in addition to, those suggested.

The Cockcroft Report (1982) included the following much-quoted paragraph:

> Mathematics teaching at all levels should include opportunities for
> – exposition by the teacher;
> – discussion between teacher and pupils and between pupils themselves;
> – appropriate practical work;
> – consolidation and practice of fundamental skills and routines;
> – problem solving, including the application of mathematics to everyday situations;
> – investigational work.

A game may well provide the stimulus for work under *all* these headings. In particular, games may help to initiate problem solving and investigational work in addition to discussion and practical work which are likely to occur when a game is being played or considered.

At the end of each chapter are *suggestions* for investigations which might arise out of a game. Some of these suggestions are followed with notes at the end of the book. Two important points need to be made:

(a) Not every investigation must have an 'answer'; the value of pursuing a particular line of thought lies in the *activity* rather than the end point (although it is nice to reach a definite conclusion sometimes!).

(b) The investigations suggested are meant to be no more than possible *starting points*, and both pupils and teachers should be able to develop many other ideas – games provide a rich source of places for beginnings.

The comments at the end of the book are often deliberately brief (or even non-existent!) and do not pursue a problem to any great depth; both teacher and pupil need freedom to follow through a problem at any depth or level, and anyway it is likely that some of the questions posed do not even have answers! Opportunities for use of skills with a computer exist in many places.

In a discussion on the objectives of mathematics teaching, Dunford (1982) argues that we must provide (a) enjoyment, (b) increase of understanding, and (c) broadening of the scope of the subject – he then proceeds to set up a case for the inclusion of games and recreations in the mathematics classroom. In relation to the games which appear in this book we might add to these objectives by including skills in investigation, analysis and logical thinking.

The philosophy put forward with great force for many years by Polya (1957) – that when stuck with a problem the would-be solver should invent a simpler one – is applicable to most investigations connected with games. Thus, for example, if *Checkers* played on a normal 8×8 board is too difficult to analyse, why not begin by considering the game played on a 2×2 board or a 3×3 board? The Open University in its mathematics foundation course (Open University 1978) has stressed an approach to investigations and problem solving which builds on the themes:

Specialise
Generalise
Conjecture
Convince

and in looking at games this sequence will often be appropriate. Thus first a special (simplified) case of a game is considered, then an attempt is made to generalise to the full game, a conjecture about the strategy for the game is made and finally an attempt to justify this strategy takes place.

Above all, games should be sources of fun and enjoyment. A bored, uninterested pupil will make a reluctant and bad investigator. It is vitally important that a game is actually *played* before it is analysed and investigated. In the chapters which follow there should be material which will be of interest both to those who just want to know about games and to those who are keen to spend some time trying to work out strategies and tactics. For both these groups of people references to other, often more detailed, books are given.

A large number of the suggestions in this book have been tried out with children in schools. Chapter 7 provides comments on children's reactions and gives examples of some of the work done. There is often no way in which a teacher can anticipate the response of pupils to a particular game or investigation; what excites one group will often produce little or no interest in another group – perhaps this is one of the main frustrations (and excitements!) of teaching. It would be false, and foolish, to claim that the games described here have all been outstanding successes with children but, for the teacher, every positive pupil response – and there should be many – is something to be treasured. Garrard (1986) writes, 'It can be easy to provide children with "open-ended" situations whereby they may engage in investigational work. You need to provide children with experiences that will help them to make full use of the opportunities investigations provide.' Games may provide some of these experiences.

2. Games of position

2.0 Introduction

Games of position have a long and varied history and fall into many different categories. For the purpose of this chapter the games considered have been divided into

Three-in-a-row games
Five-in-a-row games
Blocking games
Solitaire games.

The origins of many of the games are obscure but there is evidence that versions of some were being played 3000–4000 years ago.

2.1 Three-in-a-row games

Noughts and Crosses

The best-known game in this group is probably *Noughts and Crosses* (also know by other names, e.g. *Tic-Tac-Toe*). One advantage of the game is that it can be played with little or no equipment and needs only pencil and paper or a sandy beach, for example. The 'board' consists of four lines drawn as in Figure 2.1.

Two players play alternately. The opening player places an 'X' in any position and the opponent then places an 'O'. The aim is to get three 'X' or three 'O' symbols in a row – vertically, horizontally or diagonally. If neither player can make a row the game is drawn. The delightful simplicity of the game makes it a good vehicle for investigation.

An interesting modern variation discussed in Berlekamp, Conway and Guy (1982) is John Michon's game of *Jam*. Figure 2.2 represents eight towns joined by nine roads (numbered 1 to 9). Two players play

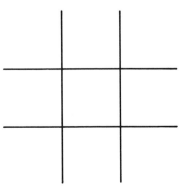

Figure 2.1

5

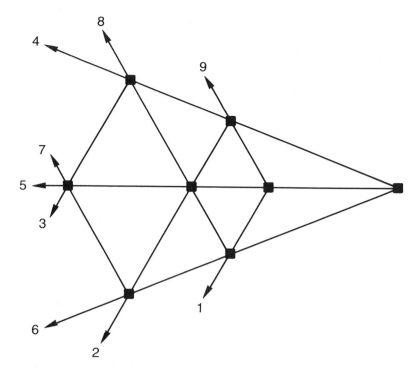

Figure 2.2

alternately and select a road at each turn. The first player to take all the roads through any town is the winner.

The numbering of the roads suggests links with a magic square of order three. The investigations at the end of the chapter may suggest further similarities.

Three Men's Morris

The board for this early form of *Noughts and Crosses* has been found cut into the roofing slabs of the ancient Egyptian temple at Kurna (c. 1400 BC). Boards have also been found in the Ptolemaic temple at Komombo (c. 300 BC), and Ovid (43 BC – AD 18) mentions the game in his *Ars Amatoria*. The Chinese played the game at the time of Confucius (c. 500 BC) under the name *Yih* (now called *Luk tsut k'i*) and there are boards cut into cathedral cloister seats in England, where the game was widely played in the fourteenth century. The game is also known as *Nine Holes* – see Brandreth (1981), for example.

The actual board is as in Figure 2.3.

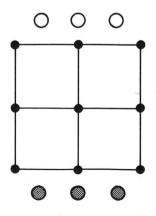

Figure 2.3

Each of the two players has three pieces ('men') of a particular colour; with alternate moves they place their pieces at any vacant point. When all the pieces have been placed, play continues by players taking turns to move a piece to a neighbouring vacant space along one of the lines. The first player to get their three pieces in a straight line is the winner. (As in *Noughts and Crosses* the line may be vertical, horizontal or diagonal.)

Achi

This game is played by schoolchildren in Ghana, the board (Figure 2.4) being marked out in the dust and each player having four distinctively coloured pebbles. Large stones marked for the game board have been found near Hadrian's wall in northern England and date from the third or fourth century AD. As in *Three Men's Morris*, pieces are introduced onto the board by alternate moves until all eight have been placed; in the second phase pieces are moved along a line to a vacant point until one player succeeds in getting three pieces in a line to win.

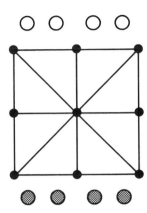

Figure 2.4

Six Men's Morris

This game was popular in Italy, France and England in the Middle Ages but appears to have become obsolete by about 1600. In this version (Figure 2.5) players have six pieces each, which are placed alternately at points of intersection of lines, with each player trying to form a row along one of the sides of either square (known as forming a *mill*). A player succeeding in getting a *mill* captures any one of the opponent's pieces and removes it from the board.

Figure 2.5

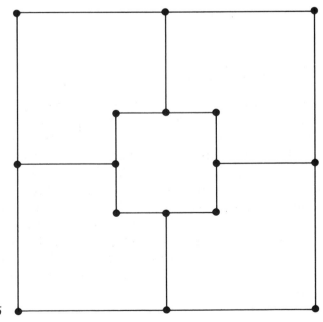

When all the pieces have been entered the game continues with players taking turns to move a piece along a line to an adjacent empty point. Once again each time a *mill* is formed an enemy piece is removed. A player loses when reduced to two pieces.

Nine Men's Morris

This is probably the best known of the 'Morris' games; boards have been found in Egypt (c. 1400 BC), Sri Lanka (c. AD 10) and in the Gokstad Viking ship (c. AD 900). During the fourteenth century elaborate boards were made in the form of shallow boxes with hinged lids – when closed one surface was used for *Chess* and the other for *Nine Men's Morris*, whilst the interior of the box was used as a *Backgammon* table. The game is similar to *Six Men's Morris*; the board is as in Figure 2.6 with each player having nine counters. Again players place pieces alternately until all are on the board; players then take turns to move a piece along a line to a neighbouring empty point. When a *mill* (three in a row) is made an opposing counter is removed but it may not be taken from an opposing *mill*. If a player is reduced to two pieces or is blocked and unable to move, they have lost the game.

Hand made 'Nine Men's Morris' board in teak and ranin from the Department of Nuclear Engineering, Oregan State University. The pieces are late XIX century in ivory and ebony.

Figure 2.6

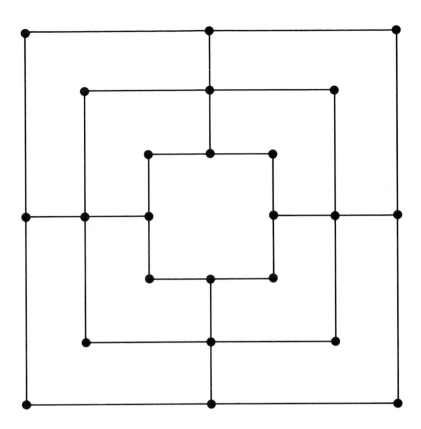

Figure 2.7

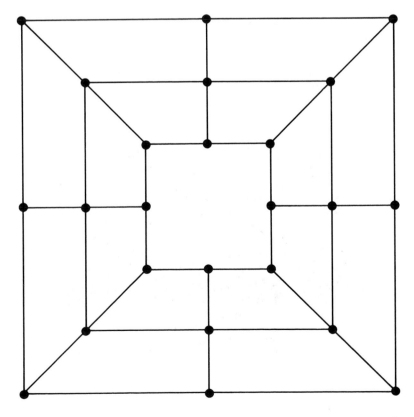

There is also a larger version of this three-in-a-row game: *Twelve Men's Morris* is played on a similar board with each player having twelve pieces. The board is as in Figure 2.7 and the rules are the same as for *Nine Men's Morris*.

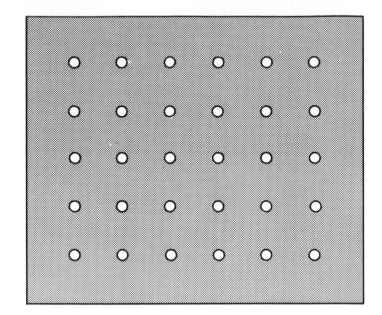

Figure 2.8

Dara

This game is played by the Dakarkari people in Nigeria and has close affinity with the 'Morris' games. The board consists of five rows of six holes (see Figure 2.8) and is usually made in the ground.

Each player has twelve distinctive pieces, usually stones, shreds of pottery or shaped sticks. These are placed one at a time in the holes in alternate turns of play. When all the pieces have been deposited the second phase begins. In this phase one piece is moved to an adjacent empty hole (not diagonally), the aim being to form a line of three pieces in a row or column (again not diagonally). When a line of three is formed the player removes any of the opponent's pieces from the board. The game ends when one player is unable to make further lines of three pieces. Lines of four do not count. Skilful placing of the pieces in the first phase is usually crucial for success in the second.

'Modern' Seega

This is a version of a traditional game played by young Egyptians today. Two players each have three pieces, which are set up on a board as in Figure 2.9.

Playing alternately, players may move a piece one or two squares in *any* direction but must not pass over another piece. The winner is the first to get three pieces in a straight line (diagonal included) other than along the original starting line.

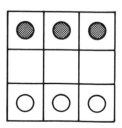

Figure 2.9

Nu Tic-Tac-Toe

This game is described and discussed in Ruderman (1985).

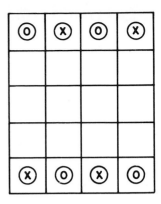

Figure 2.10

Two players take part – one with four pieces marked 'O', the other with four marked 'X' – using a board set up as shown in Figure 2.10. Moves are made alternately and, on a move, a player can push a piece to an adjacent unoccupied square (*not* diagonally). There is no jumping or capturing. The object of the game is to get three pieces in a line which may be vertical, horizontal *or* diagonal without any intervening vacant squares.

2.2   Five-in-a-row games

Traditional Seega

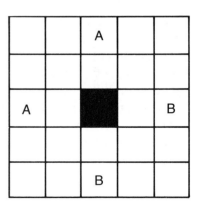

Figure 2.11

This game with a long history is still played in Egypt and provides an interesting variation on the usual 'row' games. It is played on a 5 × 5 board with the central square always empty (Figure 2.11).

Two players have stocks of pieces of different colours. The first player places two pieces anywhere on the board; the second then puts down two pieces in corresponding positions (for example, if one player plays at the squares marked A in Figure 2.11, the other follows with pieces in the squares marked B). Then, playing alternately, the players place two pieces at a time on any vacant squares. The aim is to get five pieces in a row. If neither player has won before all 24 squares are occupied then phase two of the game begins. In this phase the first player tries to replace an opponent's piece with one of their own. If a line of five is created, the first player wins. If not, the square which was tried remains empty and the second player attempts to make a line of five by the same method. If neither player can make a line of five the game is drawn.

Mulinello Quadrupio

The origin of this game is uncertain but it is described by Gelli (1900). It is played on an *Alquerque* board (see Figure 2.12 and Chapter 4 p. 41).

Each player has five pieces of a distinctive colour which are entered singly on alternate turns at any vacant point. When all have been entered a turn consists of a move along any marked line to any adjacent empty point. The winner is the first to achieve five pieces in a line.

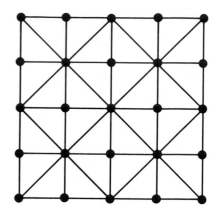

Figure *2.12*

2.3   Blocking games

Pong Hau K'i

This game, from China, is also played in Korea under the name *Ou-moul-ko-no*. It appears to be deceptively simple. Each of two players has two stones of different colours placed as in Figure 2.13. Players take it in turns to move one stone along a line to an adjacent empty point, the aim being to block the opponent's stones. There is a detailed analysis of the game in Evans (1976).

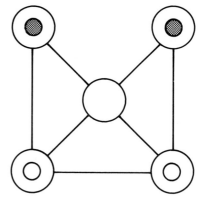

Figure *2.13*

Mu Torere

This seems to be the only board game played by the Maoris of New Zealand. The board consists of an eight-pointed star as in Figure 2.14.

Two players each have four pieces placed on adjacent points (as shown) and make alternate moves. The object of the game is to block the opponent's pieces so that they cannot move. The centre space is called the *putahi* and the eight points of the star are known as *kawai*.

A move may be:

(i) from one of the points (*kawai*) to an adjacent empty point;

(ii) from a point to the *putahi* provided that one or both of the adjacent points is occupied by an enemy piece or pieces;

(iii) from the *putahi* to a point.

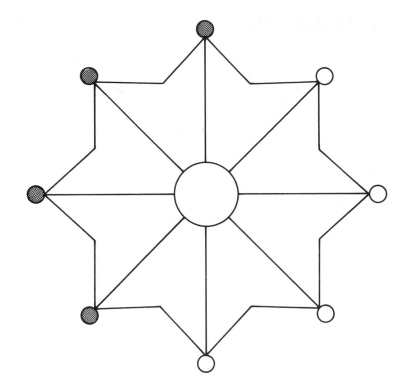

Figure 2.14

Note that not more than one piece can occupy either the *putahi* or one of the *kawai*.

Like *Pong Hau K'i* the game appears on first acquaintance to be deceptively simple.

On the west bank of the Nile near Luxor in a small chapel at Deir-el-Medina the game boards shown in Figure 2.15 are cut into massive stone slabs. The first of these could well have been for a game similar to *Mu Torere*; the other board is a mystery.

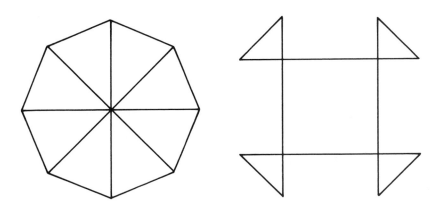

Figure 2.15

Sz' kwa (the game of four directions)

A painting on a plate by the Chinese artist Kee Fung Ng of Chinese children playing 'Sz'kwa'

The board for this Chinese children's game (Figure 2.16a) is usually marked out in the dust by the side of the road and each player has some 20 distinctive pebbles, nuts, shells, etc. At the start of the game the board is empty and each player in turn places a piece on any of the intersections. If an opponent's piece is surrounded, it is captured. Figure 2.16b shows the capture of a black piece whilst Figure 2.16c shows the capture of *two* white pieces. When a player has no counters left to place or no empty point remains where a counter can be placed without being captured, the game ends. The winner is the player holding the greater number of captured pieces.

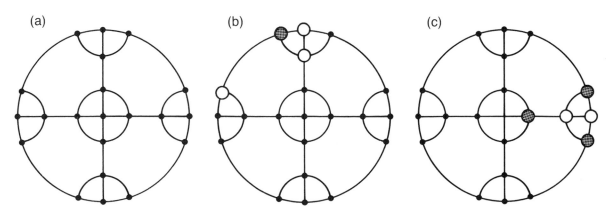

| (a) | (b) | (c) |
| Figure 2.16a | Figure 2.16b | Figure 2.16c |

There are similarities between this game and *Wei ch'i* (also known as *Go*). *Wei ch'i* is played on a square 19 × 19 board so there are 361 points instead of the 21 in *Sz'kwa* – also in the larger game the object is to capture territory and not the opponent's pieces. *Sz'kwa* appears to be a cross-and-circle game (see Chapter 5) which has been modified from being a race game to one of position.

2.4 Solitaire games

Games for one player have a particular fascination. There is no chance of profiting from the mistake of an opponent – players pit their wits against the game itself (or at least the inventor of the game!).

Pentalpha

One of the game boards cut into the roofing slabs of the temple at Kurna (c. 1700 BC) is a pentagram (see Figure 2.17). A solitaire game called *Pentalpha* is still played in Crete on a board like this.

The player has nine pebbles which must be placed onto the board as follows: a pebble is placed on any unoccupied point (the player calling 'one'), then moved through a second point, which may be occupied or unoccupied (the player calling 'two'), and then to a third empty point (the player calling 'three'). *These three points must be in a straight line.* The player repeats this 'One–two–three' move for each of the pebbles and attempts to place nine pieces on the board.

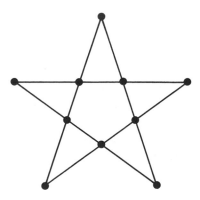

Figure 2.17

The Treble Interchange

The origin of this game is unknown. Three white and three black pieces are set up on a board as shown (Figure 2.18) with one red piece in the centre. The object of the game is to interchange the positions of the black and white pieces, with the red piece back

in the centre at the end. A
move consists of moving
first a black or white piece
and then the red piece
along a line to an adjacent
empty space. The player
continues to make these
alternate moves (i.e. a
black or white move
followed by a red) until the
interchange is complete and
the red piece is back in the
centre.

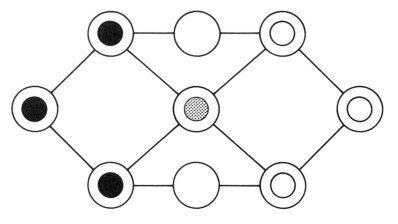

Figure *2.18*

English Solitaire

The game, or puzzle, normally known as *Solitaire* is
purported to have been invented in France in the
eighteenth century by a French nobleman in prison in
solitary confinement. It is in fact played on a board used
for the older game of *Fox and Geese* (see Chapter 4).
Solitaire has been analysed in great detail by Beasley
(1985).

An English Victorian Mahogany solitaire board with ivory peg
pieces and original round wooden box.

English Solitaire is played on a 33-hole board (see Figure 2.19). Pieces are placed in all the holes with the exception of the centre. The classic problem involves moving a piece by jumping over another piece to land in an empty place beyond (diagonal moves are not allowed). A piece jumped over is removed. The aim is to remove all the pieces except one, which should finish at the centre.

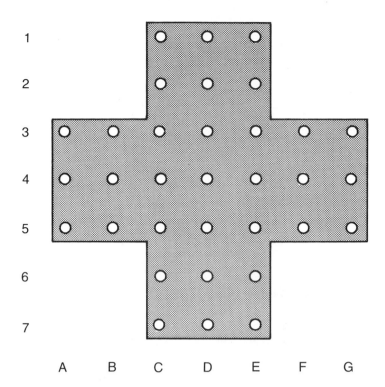

Figure *2.19*

French Solitaire

French Solitaire boards have 37 holes instead of the English 33 (see Figure 2.20).

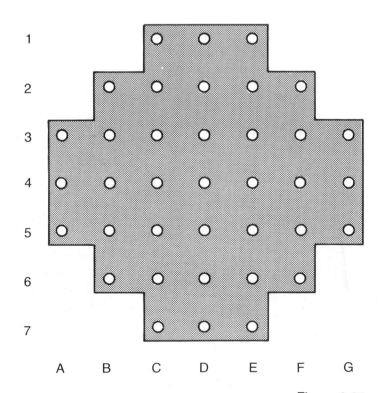

Figure *2.20*

There are many interesting and elegant problems associated with this board (again starting with a piece in every hole except the centre). For example,

The Cross of St Andrew: leave pieces as shown in Figure 2.21a.
The Professor and His Students: leave pieces as in Figure 2.21b.

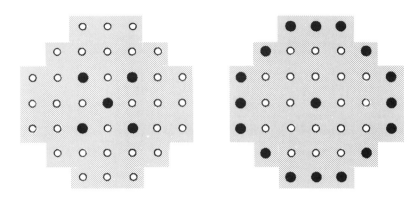

Figure *2.21a*   Figure *2.21b*

The reader interested in discovering more about *Solitaire* and associated problems is urged to consult Beasley (1985).

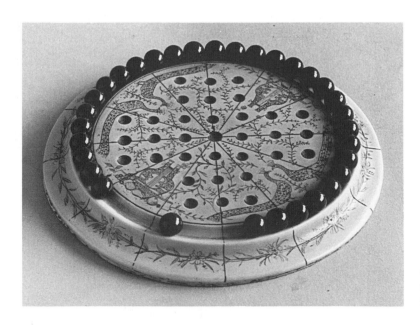

An Italian replica in composite of a scrimshaw (engraved ivory) solitaire board.

2.5 Investigations

Noughts and Crosses

(i) How many possible opening moves are there? Is there a 'best' opening move?

(ii) After each player has made one move, how many positions are possible? From which of these should the first player win?

(iii) What is the relationship between *Noughts and Crosses* and *Jam*?

(iv) A game consists of nine counters numbered 1 to 9. Two players each select a counter alternately. A player wins if the total of their counters is exactly 15. What number should the first player select? Can the game be won? If so, who should win? Investigate links with magic squares.

Three Men's Morris

(i) Who should win the game? Where should the first player play?

(ii) How many different positions are possible after all six pieces have been placed on the board?

Achi

(i) Should the first player always win?

(ii) What positions are possible after 1, 2 and 3 moves?

(iii) Is a draw possible?

Six Men's Morris

(i) Is there a 'best' opening move?

(ii) How many positions are possible after one move by each player?

(iii) What is the maximum number of pieces which can be on the board without *any* forming a row?

Nine and Twelve Men's Morris

(i) Consider questions similar to those posed for *Three Men's* and *Six Men's Morris*.

(ii) If on the boards for *Nine* and *Twelve Men's Morris* the squares are of sides 1 cm, 2 cm and 3 cm, what is the total length of the lines on each board?

(iii) If a spider were to start anywhere on the board and walk to cover all the lines, what would be the shortest possible route on each of the boards?

Dara

Consider a board with three rows of four holes. Investigate a game with four pieces each.

'Modern' Seega

(i) How many opening moves are possible?

(ii) How many positions are possible after two moves?

(iii) Is there a 'best' opening move and a 'best' reply?

Traditional Seega

(i) How many positions are possible after the first two moves?

(ii) If the board is as in Figure 2.11, what might be the best next move for player A?

Mulinello Quadrupio

(i) How many squares on the board? How many triangles?

(ii) Can the first player always win?

Pong Hau K'i

(i) How many possible positions exist in this game?

(ii) What are the best tactics for a player?

(iii) Can a win always be forced?

Mu Torere

(i) Find positions from which a win can be achieved. Should either player be able to force a draw at least?

(ii) Suggest, and invent, similar games based on a six-pointed star and its centre with three pieces each, and a four-pointed star (square) with two pieces each. Can these games be won?

Pentalpha

Find a solution and invent a suitable notation for recoding the solution.

The Treble Interchange

Can the problem be solved?

English Solitaire

Find a solution to the game. Investigate the game on a smaller board with 20 holes leaving any of the four middle holes empty at the start.

French Solitaire

Solve the problems of (i) *The Cross of St Andrew* and (ii) *The Professor and His Students*. Investigate a French-type board with 24 holes.

3. Mancala games

3.0 Introduction

Mancala is the name given to a group of games of many different forms. Strangely, in spite of a history going back several thousand years, the games have never taken root in Europe. The following brief description of one version will give an indication of the nature of a typical game.

Congklak

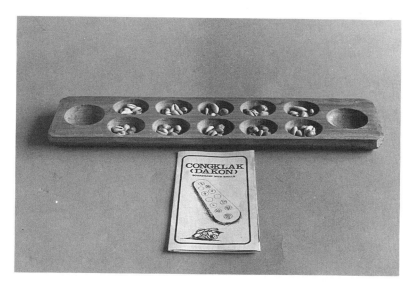

A Congklak board from Indonesia listed in the OXFAM catalogue for Christmas 1986.

This game, which comes from Indonesia, appears in the OXFAM catalogue (1987), and boards and shells may be purchased from OXFAM. The equipment is packaged by the Indonesian People's Handicraft Foundation.

The board is set up as shown in Figure 3.1; two players each have five holes (each containing five shells) and a store.

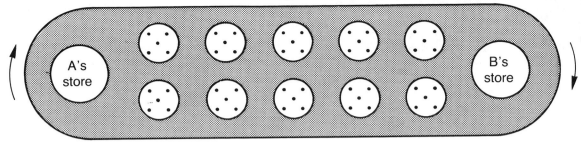

Figure 3.1

A summary of the game is as follows:

Board:	2 × 5 holes and 2 stores
Pieces:	50 shells
Distribution:	5 shells in each hole
Direction:	Clockwise
Move:	Several sowings
Game:	The winner is the player with most shells in their store at the end of the game.

Players play alternately and, at a turn, a player 'lifts' the shells from any hole on their own side of the board and 'sows' them one at a time into holes going clockwise round the board (including the player's own store but not the opponent's). If the last shell falls in a loaded hole, the shells are lifted from that hole and the sowing continues. If the last shell falls in an empty hole on the opponent's side, the turn ends. If the last shell falls in an empty hole on the player's side, then the shells in the opponent's hole opposite (if any) are captured and put in the player's store. The opponent then plays. If the last shell lands in the store, the turn ends.

Here is how one game might start. The starting position is

```
        5  5  5  5  5
     0                 0
        5  5  5  5  5
```

Player A decides to sow from the middle hole to get

```
   6  6  5  5  5                6  0  6  6  6
 1                0   and then 1                0
   6  6  0  5  5                6  6  1  6  6
```

Thus A captures the 6 shells opposite the 1, and now B plays.

23

The game ends when one player has no shells left on their side; the opponent then adds any shells left on the board to their own store. The winner is the player with most shells in their store at the end of the game. Mancala games are widely disseminated over tropical and subtropical areas of Africa, Asia and the adjacent islands, while African slaves took them to the West Indies and the Americas. There are three basic forms of the game, played with two rows (*Congklak* is an example), three rows, and four rows of holes. These will be referred to as Mancala II, Mancala III and Mancala IV. The most popular and widest spread form is Mancala II whilst the rarest form is Mancala III which is found only in a restricted area – North East Africa and Arabia.

The earliest known Mancala board (c. 1580–1150 BC), with two rows of holes, was found in Egypt. There is a board cut into the floor of the portico of the temple of Hephaistos in Athens but when it was made is not known – possibly in ancient Greece or even as late as the Turkish occupation of Athens from 1458 to 1833. Boards appeared in Sri Lanka during the early centuries AD and in Arabia before the time of Muhammad. There are several well-cut sets of holes in the temple of Kurna in Egypt, and others at the temples of Karnak and Luxor. The best set at Kurna has 16 holes and is about 60 cm long with holes approximately 6 cm wide and 2 cm deep.

In Syria, Egypt and West Africa, Mancala II is played by all sections of the community but usually men with men, women with women, and children with children. In Southern India, Sri Lanka, Malaysia, Indonesia and the Philippines it is mainly a woman's game. In Sri Lanka it is usually played at New Year, and in the West Indies there is a religious significance attached, the game sometimes being played to amuse the spirit of the dead awaiting burial. Making boards is thought to involve spiritual danger and only old men who have lost a wife make them. The game is often played in holes dug in the ground or cut in outcrops of rock by the roadside.

The word 'Mancala' is taken from *Mankalah*, a version played in Egypt using holes dug in the sand and pebbles or pellets of camel's dung. The ready availability of equipment makes Mancala games ideal for playing on a holiday beach. Mancala games lend themselves easily to interesting analysis, and endless possible investigations could be carried out at many different levels of mathematical sophistication. Equipment needed is simple and easily improvised; peas, coins, pebbles, matchsticks,

. . . all make suitable pieces, and a board can be made from egg cartons, baking tins or a piece of wood. A 'live' game could be played with children forming the pieces and circles drawn on a school playground the holes. Mancala games provide a good challenge for a computer programmer – the pattern of play lends itself well to a computer simulation and it is usually not difficult to write a simple program to play a game. (An example of an attempt to computerise a game and provide a good display of the board can be found in Bishop (1987).) The games described below illustrate some of the wide variety of forms of Mancala.

3.1   Mancala II games

In its basic form a board for Mancala II is a piece of wood with two rows of holes cut into one side. In Egypt there are six holes per row, in Syria seven and in some children's games as few as three. In a Masai game there are as many as fifty.

To facilitate description the notation shown in Figure 3.2, for an anticlockwise game, is used. Moves are denoted by, for example, Y3e, meaning that player Y lifts 3 pieces from hole e and sows anticlockwise.

Player Y

f	e	d	c	b	a
A	B	C	D	E	F

Player X

Figure 3.2

Mankal'ah L'ib Al-Ghashim (The game of the unlearned)

Board:	2 × 6 holes
Pieces:	72 cowries or pebbles
Distribution:	Haphazard in the players' six holes
Direction:	Anticlockwise
Move:	Several laps
Game:	Until one player has won 60 shells

This game is described by Lane (1890) in an account written in Egypt between 1833 and 1835. At the start one of the players distributes the 72 pieces into the holes putting at least 4 in each. The other has the choice of either starting or turning the board round. Players always play from their extreme right-hand hole (i.e. in Figure 3.2, F for X, f for Y) or if that is empty from the hole nearest to it. If the last seed sown drops into an empty hole, the turn ends; if it falls into a hole which now contains 2 or 4 seeds, then those pieces and the pieces in the hole immediately opposite are captured, together with those from the immediately preceding holes containing 2 or 4 pieces and the pieces in their opposite holes. If a player finishes with any other number in the last hole after sowing, the seeds are taken out and sown as before until either a capture is made or the last piece falls into an empty hole.

As an example, suppose at the start of a game the pieces are distributed as follows:

$$6 \quad 7 \quad 5 \quad 4 \quad 9 \quad 8$$
$$9 \quad 5 \quad 4 \quad 6 \quad 4 \quad 5$$

Play proceeds:

1	X5F	2	X8e	3	X10a	
4	X6E	(X captures 2 from e and 7 from B)				
5	Y8f	6	Y13b	7	Y9c	8 Y5F
9	Y3e	(Y captures 4 from B and 0 from e)				

The position is now:

$$3 \quad 0 \quad 11 \quad 1 \quad 2 \quad 4$$
$$15 \quad 0 \quad 9 \quad 11 \quad 3 \quad 0$$

and the game proceeds:

10	X3E	11	X3b	(turn ends in empty hole)
12	Y3f	13	Y10C	
14	Y17A	(Y captures 4 from F and 7 from a)		
15	X3E			
16	X3b	(X captures 4 from e and 3 from B)		
17	Y2f	(turn ends in empty hole)		
18	X1F	(X captures 2 from a)		

This leaves the position:

$$0 \quad 0 \quad 15 \quad 5 \quad 0 \quad 0$$
$$2 \quad 1 \quad 2 \quad 14 \quad 0 \quad 0$$

and so on . . .

It quickly becomes apparent that the players are forced into their moves by the initial arrangement and all moves are predetermined once the board has been set up – hence the tag 'unlearned' on the name!

Leab El-Akil (The game of the wise or intelligent)

This game is exactly the same as the previous one except that: (i) at the start the end holes on each side are normally left empty, and (ii) a player may begin at *any* hole. The choice of lifting from any loaded hole makes the game a much more skilful contest.

Cups

Although Mancala games have never become popular in Europe and the Western world, attempts have been made to introduce variants. A game called *Cups* is outlined by Sackson (1969). The board is set up as in Figure 3.3.

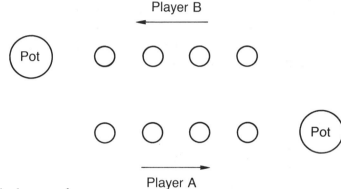

Each player has 40 counters and players play alternately. At a turn a player can either:

(a) take 1, 2, 3 or 4 counters and place them in the player's own cups – the first counter goes in the left-hand cup and subsequent counters one at a time in cups to the right; or

(b) take the contents of one of the existing cups and sow the counters one at a time to the right so that the last counter lands in the 'Pot'. (Thus the chosen cup must contain the exact number of counters required.)

Counters are captured when a player plays such that the last counter lands in an empty cup; the contents (if any) of the opponent's opposite cup are then captured and placed in the player's own 'Pot'. The player with the most counters at the end is the winner.

It is easy to see that if a player has more counters in a cup than the number required to reach the 'Pot' by sowing, then that cup is blocked and cannot be emptied unless the pieces are captured by the opponent.

Wari

This is a well-known game in which two players each
have six cups containing four counters (or seeds) apiece.

Board:	2 × 6 holes
Pieces:	48 seeds
Distribution:	4 seeds in each cup
Direction:	Anticlockwise
Move:	One sowing
Game:	Player with most seeds at end is the winner.

Player B

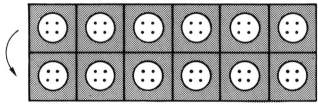

Player A

Figure 3.4

A and B play alternately, lifting the seeds from one of
the holes on their side of the board and 'sowing' one into
each hole in an anticlockwise direction. If the last seed
drops into an enemy hole to make a final total of 2 or 3,
the seeds are captured and the seeds of any unbroken
sequence of 2's and 3's on the opponent's side of the
board adjacent to and behind the plundered hole are also
taken. The player holding most seeds at the end is the
winner.

If a hole becomes heavily loaded then sowing may
require more than one cycle of the board; in this case the
emptied cup is omitted from sowing in the second and
subsequent cycles. If all an opponent's cups are empty a
player must, if possible, move a piece to the opponent's
half of the board. Also a player is not allowed to capture
all the opponent's seeds (this would prevent the
opponent moving on the next turn) – instead the player
must leave intact any one cup.

As an illustration of a move, if at some stage the
position is:

B: 1   2   1   1   2   2

A: 4   4   2   7   1   0

and A empties the hole containing 7 seeds, the position becomes:

$$\text{B:} \quad 1 \quad 3 \quad 2 \quad 2 \quad 3 \quad 3$$
$$\text{A:} \quad 4 \quad 4 \quad 2 \quad 0 \quad 2 \quad 1$$

and A captures $3 + 2 + 2 + 3 + 3 = 13$ seeds.

Kalah

Haggerty (1985) gives an account of a game called *Kalah*. It is, he claims, the 'only game continuously played in widely separated parts of the world on at least three continents from the time of the first civilised country, Sumeria, down to the present'. The game is very similar to *Congklak*. Two players each have six holes and a store, and each hole contains either three (for beginners) or six pebbles at the start. The rules differ from *Congklak* in the following ways: (i) sowing is anticlockwise; (ii) there is no resowing; (iii) a player continues only if the last pebble sown lands in their own store, when they can start again from any of their holes. Capturing occurs as in *Congklak* when a turn finishes in an empty hole on a player's own side.

Haggerty reports that in Boston, Los Angeles, Cleveland, Chicago and New York playgrounds are equipped with this game. He goes on to state, '*Kalah* is the best all-round teaching aid in the country'. He backs up this claim with the comment that *Kalah* is purely mathematical, no element of chance enters into it and the basic rules are so simple that even a young pre-school child can play the game. The game has also been called *Pits and Pebbles* – the stores are referred to as 'kalah'. In an article published with that by Haggerty, Brill (1985) gives details of 'a project for the low-budget mathematics laboratory' – the construction of the equipment needed for *Kalah* using cardboard, glue, paper cups and tape.

3.2 Mancala III and Mancala IV games

These forms of Mancala are far less common than Mancala II. Mancala III is the rarest form and was thought to be obsolete but Pankhurst (1971) records that there are several varieties played in Ethiopia of which the following is an example.

Gabata

Board:	3 × 6 cups
Pieces:	54 pebbles
Distribution:	3 pebbles per cup
Direction:	Anticlockwise
Move:	1. Race between players
	2. Several laps
Game:	Player with most pebbles wins.

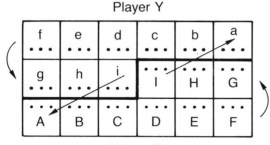

Figure 3.5

The game begins with a board as shown in Figure 3.5. Both players begin together, sowing from their left-hand back hole. Player X follows the route ABCDEFGHIabcdefghiA . . . and player Y the route abcdefghiABCDEFGHIa . . . Pebbles are resown from the last hole of a sowing until one player finishes in an empty hole. (Thus phase one of the game is really a race between the players.) The first player to come to a halt begins phase two. In this phase a player starts from any one of their own holes and sows and resows until landing in an empty hole. When this occurs on the player's own side of the board, opponent's pieces in the same column are captured (for example, landing in C, a player would capture pieces in i and d). The player then lifts the single pebble and sows into the next hole and continues as before until the turn ends by landing in an enemy empty hole or in one of the player's own empty holes faced by empty enemy holes.

30

Kiarabu

A four rank mancala board from Zaire. The board is old and has been repaired in several places.

Mancala IV is played in East and South Africa and stone boards found in Zimbabwe date from somewhere between AD 1400 and 1800. The earliest mention of the game is contained in a book *De Ludis Orientalis Libro Duo* published in 1694. It is often entirely a man's game. The following is a game from Zanzibar called *Kiarabu*.

Board:	4 × 8 cups
Pieces:	96 seeds
Distribution:	3 seeds per cup
Direction:	Either clockwise or anticlockwise
Move:	Several laps
Game:	Player with most seeds at the end wins.

Player Y

h	g	f	e	d	c	b	a
• • •	• • •	• • •	• • •	• • •	• • •	• • •	• • •
i	j	k	l	m	n	o	p
• • •	• • •	• • •	• • •	• • •	• • •	• • •	• • •
P	O	N	M	L	K	J	I
• • •	• • •	• • •	• • •	• • •	• • •	• • •	• • •
A	B	C	D	E	F	G	H

Player X

Figure 3.6

31

The board is set up as shown in Figure 3.6 with 3 seeds in each hole. Players play entirely in their own holes (nearest two rows, referred to as front and back with the back being nearest the player). A move begins from *any* of a player's holes, and each move may be either completely clockwise or completely anticlockwise. The seeds from the chosen hole are sown and resown until the move ends when the last seed lands in an empty hole. If this hole is a back hole, the turn ends. If it is a front hole and if the opponent's front hole in the same file (e.g. k if player X finishes in hole N) contains seeds, then these are captured together with seeds in the opponent's back hole (e.g. f). But if the opponent's front hole is empty, nothing is won.

When one player has only single pieces in holes and empty holes, the game ends and the player who moved last takes any seeds left on the board.

3.3 Solitaire games

Some Mancala games are in a form for a single player.

Ise-Ozin-Egbe

Board:	2 × 3 holes
Pieces:	22 beans
Distribution:	as in Figure 3.7
Direction:	Clockwise
Move:	Several laps
Game:	Player attempts to return to original position.

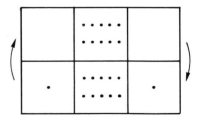

Figure 3.7

The game comes from Nigeria. The player begins by lifting the 10 beans in the bottom row and sowing. Subsequent moves begin from the hole at which the previous sowing finishes; the aim is to arrive back at the original position. Seemingly a rather dull game! Egharevba (1949) showed that the initial arrangement repeats after 144 moves – a short computer program helps considerably in confirming this fact.

Tchuka Ruma

An East Indian game, *Tchuka Ruma* (Degrazia, 1949) gives a challenge similar to *Ise-Ozin-Egbe*. Figure 3.8 shows the board at the start of the game.

Figure *3.8*

Here pieces are taken from any cup and sown from left to right – if the Ruma is reached with more than one piece in hand then the sowing continues at the extreme left-hand hole. If the last cup sown is empty you lose; if not you sow again (starting from the hole in which you finished). If the sowing ends in the Ruma you may select any cup to begin the next move. The aim is to get all the pieces in the Ruma.

A variation of *Tchuka Ruma* involves a circular arrangement of a bowl and cups (Figure 3.9; Averbach and Chein, 1980). The rules are the same. You sow from any cup but lose if the last piece drops into an empty cup. If the last piece drops into the bowl you may restart anywhere. The aim is to get all the pieces into the bowl. Play is usually clockwise.

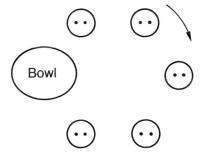

Figure *3.9*

Investigations

Mancala II

An African wood carving of a
game of mancala.

Mancala games give rise to some complex analysis. It is
perhaps easier to examine simplified versions before trying
to produce strategies and analyses for games like *Wari* and
Leab El-Akil. Indeed many versions of Mancala do have
children's games where the numbers of cups and seeds
are reduced.

(i) Suppose a game is started with:

$$2 \quad 2 \quad 2$$

$$2 \quad 2 \quad 2$$

and two players play alternately, sowing anticlockwise
from *any* cup, with the winner being the first to achieve
five seeds in any hole. Who should win and how?
   It is easier to represent the seeds in one line, viz.

$$2 \quad 2 \quad 2 \quad 2 \quad 2 \quad 2$$

Player A leaves:

$$0 \quad 3 \quad 3 \quad 2 \quad 2 \quad 2$$

It is not difficult to show that player B will win if they
now sow from any hole except the one on the extreme
right.

There are many variations possible for such a simple game.

(ii) Start with:

$$3 \quad 3 \quad 3$$
$$3 \quad 3 \quad 3$$

The winner is the first to leave *seven* seeds in any hole.

(iii) Begin with:

$$4 \quad 4 \quad 4$$
$$4 \quad 4 \quad 4$$

Try to be the first to get *nine* in one cup.

Mankal'ah L'ib Al-Ghasim

This game can be played in a simplified form. Consider a board with 2×2 holes, played with 12 seeds, with at least 2 in each cup at the start. Remember that a player can either accept the opponent's board setting or turn the board round, and that a capture is initiated if the final seed sown leaves a total of 2 or 4.

(i) Would you accept:

Opponent

$$2 \qquad 5$$
$$3 \qquad 2$$

You

at the start? Or would you let your opponent begin by turning the board round?

(ii) How many arrangements of this small board are possible? How many of these should you accept (and so begin) with the expectation of winning?

Extensions which come immediately to mind include increasing the number of seeds on a 2×2 board and increasing the size of the board whilst varying the number of seeds.

(iii) How many games are possible on the original 2×6 board with 72 pebbles and at least 4 per hole?

Cups

Suppose a game of *Cups* consists of two cups and a pot for each player; players have ten counters each and can place one or two counters in a move.

What is the best opening move?

Which player should win?

Kalah

Investigate positions after one move by each player. Since there is no 'luck' in the game, is it possible to work out a winning sequence of moves for either player?

Gabata

(i) Suppose two players play phase one of the game at exactly the same speed; investigate what happens.
(ii) If player X makes two distinct sowings for every one made by Y, what happens?
(iii) A simplified game could be played on a board with three rows of 2 cups. Suppose on a 3×2 board X is left with the position:

0 1

5 5

1 6

How did this position arise?
Should X now start sowing from the 1, 6 or 5 in the next phase?
(iv) Invent a position where X can capture 17 pieces (i.e. all except the last one sown). How many such positions can be found?

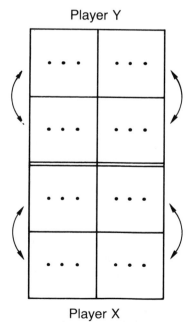

Player Y

Player X

Figure *3.10*

Kiriabu

(i) Consider a simplified board as in Figure 3.10. Where would you start as player X? What happens? (Remember you can choose to move clockwise or anticlockwise on each sowing.)
(ii) If you are X and it is your turn, what is the best move from the position in Figure 3.11?
(iii) Invent a position with all 96 pieces on the board from which X can play and win without Y having a move.

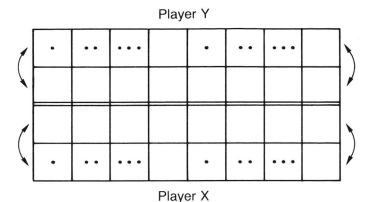

Player Y

Player X

Figure *3.11*

Ise-Ozin-Egbe

  (i) What is the maximum number of pieces to appear in one hole during a game?

 (ii) Try different arrangements of seeds or different starting points. For example:

How long before

1	1	1	or	2	2	2
1	1	1		2	2	2

repeat?

How long before arrangements such as:

1	2	1	and	1	3	1
1	2	1		1	3	1

repeat?

(iii) Find arrangements which repeat in the smallest possible number of moves.

Tchuka Ruma

  (i) Find a solution to Tchuka Ruma. How many solutions are possible?

 (ii) What about different numbers of holes and pieces?
     e.g. 6 holes and a Ruma with 3 pieces per hole,
        8 holes and a Ruma with 4 pieces per hole.

(iii) The game with a circular arrangement of cups is open to the same investigations as *Tchuka Ruma*, the number of cups and pieces per cup being varied as before. Investigate whether the game can be completed with different numbers of cups and pieces per cup.

Some other possible 'solitaire' investigations

Suppose three single seeds are placed in a row:

$$1 \quad 1 \quad 1$$

how many sowings (starting where you like each time and continuing at the extreme left when the right hand end is reached) are needed to get all the seeds in one place? It is not difficult here to see that the best sequence needs three moves:

$$1 \quad 1 \quad 1$$
$$1 \quad 0 \quad 2$$
$$0 \quad 1 \quad 2$$
$$0 \quad 0 \quad 3$$

If we now take four single seeds:

$$1 \quad 1 \quad 1 \quad 1$$

then at least four moves are needed, for example,

$$0 \quad 2 \quad 1 \quad 1$$
$$0 \quad 2 \quad 0 \quad 2$$
$$0 \quad 0 \quad 1 \quad 3$$
$$0 \quad 0 \quad 0 \quad 4$$

What about 5, 6, 7, 8, . . . single seeds? What is the least number of moves needed to get all the seeds in one place? Can any pattern be found?

What about 3, 4, 5, . . . cups with 2 seeds each? Or higher numbers in each?

4 • War games

4.0 Introduction

Many games are in the form of wars between armies. In this chapter the games are divided into two broad categories:

  (i) wars between equal forces,
  (ii) wars between unequal forces.

The games described all depend on the skills and strategies of the players involved and the only element of chance lies in the actual structure of the games themselves. Analysis reveals that, in some games, a particular player (e.g. the one who starts) should win if no mistakes are made but outcomes rarely depend on the throw of a die or toss of a coin or the equivalent. The origins of war games frequently lie in real life; players have the opportunity to fight battles without the anxiety of human losses!

4.1 Games between equal forces

There are two distinct types of games involving equal forces and these can be put into broad categories labelled 'Chess' and 'Draughts' (or 'Checkers').

'Chess' games

Chess itself is a relatively late board game whose origins can be traced back to about the sixth century AD in India, but its roots lie very clearly in a game called *Shaturanga*. The board from an ancient Indian race game, *Ashtapada*, was used in the fifth century for

Shaturanga, a battle game involving four armies in a miniature battle between four kingdoms, two allied against the other two (black and red against yellow and green). It was played on an 8 × 8 board (Figure 4.1).

Red

S	P			R	E	H	S
H	P			P	P	P	P
E	P						
R	P						
						P	R
						P	E
P	P	P	P			P	H
S	H	E	R			P	S

Yellow (left)   Green (right)   Black (bottom)

Figure 4.1

Each player controlled an army of a particular colour consisting of eight pieces: a Rajah (R), a Horse (H) representing cavalry, a Ship (S) representing boatmen, an Elephant (E) representing elephant troops, and four Pawns (P) representing infantry. The board was set up initially as shown in the figure. A decision about which piece would move was made by throwing a 'long' die with 2, 3, 4 and 5 on its faces (see Figure 4.2), with moves being made by the Ship with a 2, the Horse with a 3, the Elephant with a 4 and either the Rajah or a Pawn with a 5.

The Rajah moved like a King in *Chess*, the Elephant like a Rook and the Horse like a Knight. Ships moved two squares diagonally and could jump over an intervening piece. Pawns moved as in *Chess* (including diagonal capture but not a possible two square advance on the first move). Capturing was as in *Chess* but Pawns and Ships could only capture each other – these pieces were minor pieces whilst the others were major pieces. The detailed rules can be found in Bell (1973) but the basic aim is to capture all the opposing armies.

Shaturanga was played largely as a gambling game but when gambling was forbidden in the Hindu culture, the gambling laws were evaded by discarding the die and allowing choice of the piece to be moved. (*Shaturanga* was specifically mentioned in the Ninth Book of the Laws of Manu as being illegal and players were liable to incur corporal punishment.) Eventually the game became one for just two players with the allied forces being amalgamated – this is why we have the duplication of pieces in the game of *Chess*.

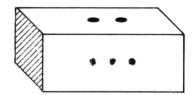

Figure 4.2

Shaturanga developed into a game called *Shatranj* which was played in Persia before AD 600. The pieces became a King, Prime Minister, Elephant, War Horse, Ruhk ('Rook' which developed out of the 'Ship') and Pawns. The Prime Minister eventually became the Queen with increased power of movement, making it the most powerful piece on the board as in modern *Chess*.

'Draughts' games

The earliest game in this family appears to be *Alquerque* which probably dates back to 1400 BC in the Middle East. The game moved westwards and an Arabic game called *Quirkat* reached Spain via the invasion of the Moors to become *El-quirkat* before it was finally recorded under its Spanish name *Alquerque* in about AD 1250. The board for *Alquerque* is shown in Figure 4.3.

Two players each have 12 pieces (black and white) and make alternate moves from the initial arrangement shown in the figure. Moves are along a line to an adjacent point. Pieces are captured by being jumped over – more than one capture being possible in a move. These rules from a thirteenth century Spanish manuscript are incomplete and additional rules (for example, preventing backward moves) are needed before a proper game can be played.

Modern *Draughts* is basically the same game as *Alquerque* but with the promotion of pieces being possible. The actual game of *Draughts* seems to have come from France in about AD 1100; this game was played on an 8 × 8 board with 12 pieces for each player. Variations include Continental or Polish games on 10 × 10 boards and French, Canadian or Singaporean games on 12 × 12 boards.

Other games played on the 8 × 8 board include, for example, a game called *Reversi*, invented in England in 1888 and recently revived under the name *Othello*.

Another game, *Sixteen Soldiers*, played in Sri Lanka and Southern India, follows the rules of *Alquerque* exactly but is played on the board shown in Figure 4.4. (This board is also used for a game called *Cows and Leopards* – see below.) Each player has sixteen pieces, placed initially as shown. Players move alternately and can move in any direction along a line to an adjacent

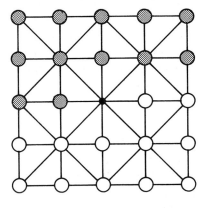

Figure 4.3

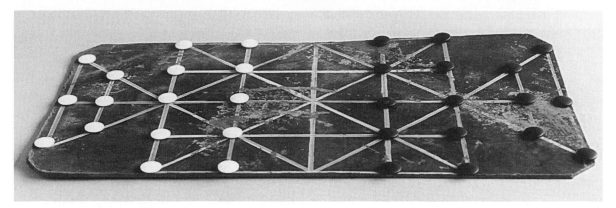

A board for 'Sixteen Soldiers' which belonged to a patrol of Malaysian police near Penang.

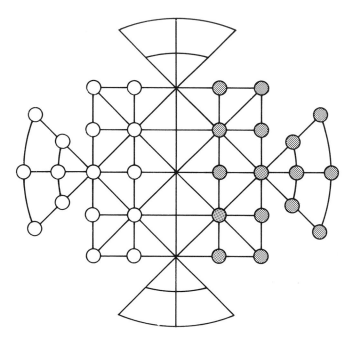

Figure *4.4*

point. A capture is made by jumping over an enemy piece to a vacant point beyond – several pieces can be captured in one move by a series of leaps over single enemy pieces. A player loses when all their pieces have been captured. As an additional rule it is suggested that if a player fails to make a capture, the piece is 'huffed' and removed from the board. A variant gives each player seven extra pieces, placed on the points of the triangle to the player's left.

A smaller version with the name *Lau Kati Kata*, played in Bengal, gives each player six pieces and uses the board in Figure 4.5.

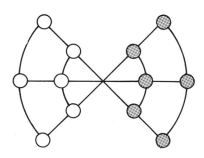

Figure *4.5*

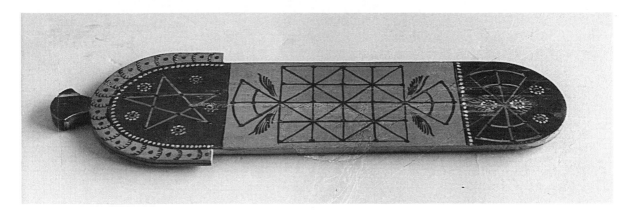

The underside of the lid of a compendium of eight games from Madras. The boards are marked for 'Pentalpha', 'Cows and Leopards' and 'Lau Kati Kata'.

4.2 Games involving unequal forces

These games usually involve a small force (sometimes only one piece) fighting a larger force but with the former having greater freedom of movement. It is common for human sympathy to lie with the underdog and hence the greatest satisfaction is often obtained in leading the smaller 'army' to victory. In 'unequal force' games it is interesting and instructive to vary the sizes of the forces and consider the effect – most games that have survived enjoy a delicate balance between opposing forces and even slight changes often produce a very uneven contest.

The Maharajah and the Sepoys

This game is played on a chessboard and provides a contest between a *Maharajah* (the ruler of an Indian state) and *Sepoys* (Indian soldiers). One player (white) sets up 16 chess pieces as for a normal game (Figure 4.6); these pieces move as in Chess. The other player (black) has only one piece which may be placed at any square on the board and has the power of movement of both a Queen and a Knight. The white pieces are the Sepoys and the black piece the Maharajah. The aim is for either the Maharajah to checkmate the white King or the white pieces to checkmate the Maharajah.

White, if never leaving a piece unsupported, should win but any error is likely to leave black, with great mobility, the chance of trapping white's King.

Black

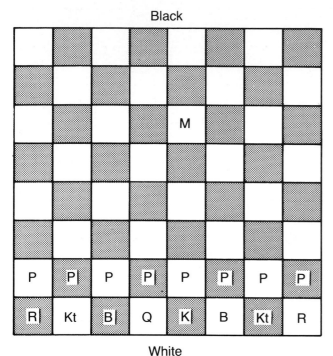

White

Figure *4.6*

Tablut

School pupils playing 'Tablut'. The board is made of five-ply with inlaid marquetry squares, the pieces are made of sheep's bone.

This game has its origin in Lapland and was described by the Swedish botanist Carolus Linnaeus in 1732 in a diary he kept as a young student travelling through Lapland. (Linnaeus established principles for naming and classifying plants and animals – a modification of his system is still used today.) *Tablut* is a fascinating and well-balanced contest which calls for careful and thoughtful analysis by both players. One player has 8 blond Swedish soldiers and a King, and the other has 16 dark Muscovites. All pieces can move any number of squares in a straight line (cf. Rook in *Chess*). The 9 × 9 board is set up initially as shown in Figure 4.7.

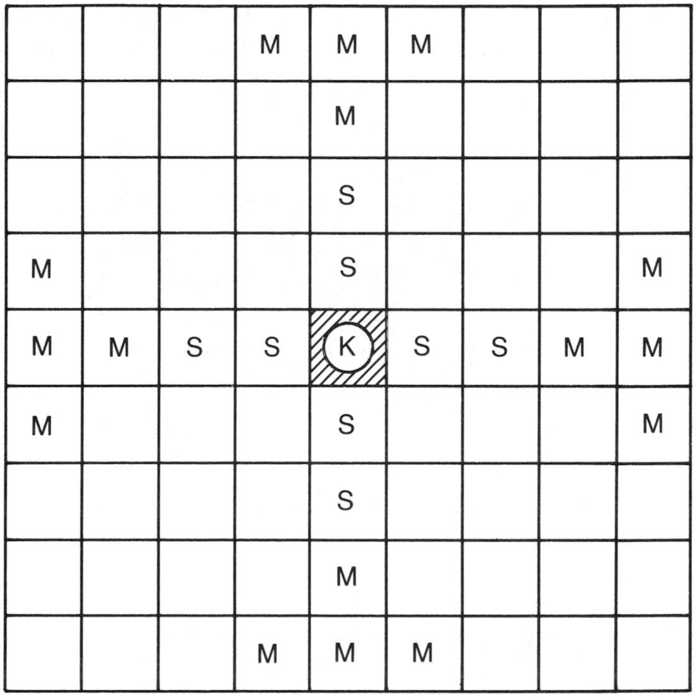

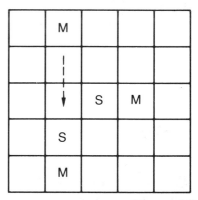

Figure 4.7

Players move alternately and a piece is captured when opposing pieces occupy both adjacent squares in a row or column – this is called the 'custodian' method of capture. In Figure 4.8 the capture of two Swedes is illustrated. However, a piece can move unharmed onto an unoccupied space between two enemy pieces. The central square is called the *konakis* (throne) and can be occupied only by the King. The King is captured, and the Muscovites win, if all four squares around the King are occupied by enemy pieces or if the King is surrounded on three sides and the fourth is the *konakis*. If the King reaches any square on the perimeter of the board, the Swedes win.

Figure 4.8

Fox and Geese

There are many forms of this game which probably originates from Northern Europe in the fourteenth century – it is mentioned in a work from Iceland written about AD 1300. In one of the simplest forms, one player has 13 geese and the other a fox. The board is as in Figure 4.9.

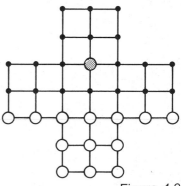

Figure 4.9

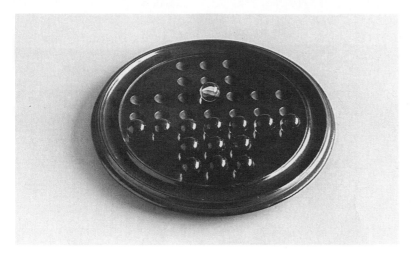

An English XVIII century mahogany 'Fox and Geese' board arranged for the start of a game with 13 geese (black marbles) and a fox (coloured marble). The marbles are modern replacements.

Players move alternately and both fox and geese can move along a line to an adjacent point. If the fox jumps over a goose (not diagonally) the goose is killed and removed from the board. (Two or more geese can be killed in one move by a series of jumps over single pieces by the fox.) The geese cannot jump over the fox but instead try to crowd him into a corner, making movement impossible. The fox wins if he can deplete the geese so that they cannot trap him. If the geese are played correctly they should always win. In a later form of the game, aimed at improving the chances of the fox, 17 geese were used but they were limited to forward and sideways movement (Figure 4.10).

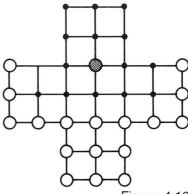

Figure *4.10*

There is another game commonly referred to as *Fox and Geese*. It is played on a *Checkers* board as shown in Figure 4.11. The geese can move only diagonally *forward* one square at a time. The fox can move diagonally one square at a time in *any* direction. No capturing or jumping is allowed and the fox tries to break through the geese whilst the geese try to trap the fox. This version is analysed and discussed in detail in Berlekamp, Conway and Guy (1982).

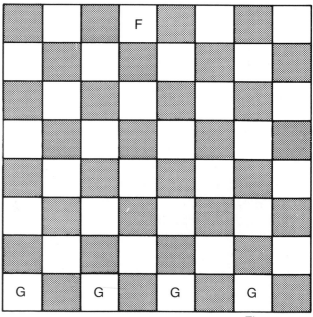

Figure *4.11*

There is a series of games similar to *Fox and Geese* which come mostly from Southern Asia and seem to be independent of the Scandinavian games. They involve a variety of other animals, are usually played on a variation of a Solitaire board and involve a powerful animal or bird, represented in small numbers, fighting against a more vulnerable one with a larger number of pieces.

Lambs and Tigers

This is a game played by Hindu children in India. One player has 3 tigers and the other 15 lambs. Pieces are placed alternately on the board (Figure 4.12) for three moves, the tigers being placed on the points marked 'T'. Thereafter a tiger may be moved to an adjacent point after each lamb is placed. Lambs can only move after all 15 have been introduced. A tiger 'kills' a lamb by jumping over it – several single lambs may be killed by a series of jumps in one move. The tigers seek to destroy all the lambs whilst the lambs try to hem in the tigers so that they cannot move.

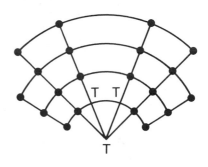

Figure 4.12

Cows and Leopards

In this game, from Southern Asia, 2 leopards attack 24 cows. The board (Figure 4.13) is the same as that for *Sixteen Soldiers* (see above) and the rules are the same as for *Lambs and Tigers* except that the leopards can be placed on *any* points at the start. The cows should always succeed in trapping the leopards.

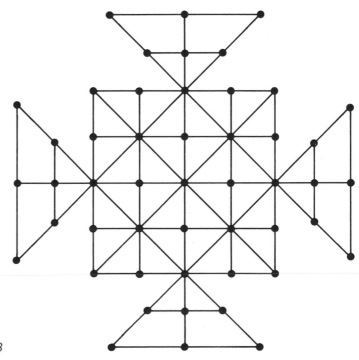

Figure 4.13

47

The first four moves of 'Cows and Leopards' on a reproduction board.

Vultures and Crows

Also called *Kaooa*, this game comes from India. It uses the *Pentalpha* board (see chapter 2; Figure 4.14) and involves one vulture against seven crows. The rules of movement and capture are the same as those in the two previous games. A crow is first entered, then the vulture, a second crow is entered, the vulture now moves one space, and so on until all the crows are on the board – then the crows and vultures move alternately, with the vulture making captures by jumping over crows.

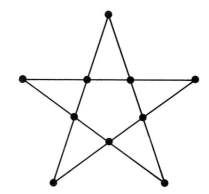

Figure *4.14*

The New Military Game of German Tactics

The game dates from about 1870 and probably refers to the Franco-Prussian war. It provides a good example of the development of a game from existing, older games. The board (Figure 4.15) is similar to that for *Fox and Geese*, the balance of forces is exactly that of *Cows and Leopards*. One player has 2 officers, the other 24 men.

The men are placed at the points marked with black circles and the officers can be placed at any points within the 'garrison' (enclosed by a thick line). The men move first – a single piece is moved one space forwards or sideways. The officers are free to move one space in any direction and can capture men by jumping over them. The men win by taking possession of the nine garrison points – the officers win by reducing the men to eight or (surprisingly) by both or one of them being blockaded in the garrison so that they cannot move.

Love (1979) describes a game, *Transvaal*, played on an identical board. The game commemorates the siege of Ladysmith in the Boer War (1899–1902) and is played with 2 soldiers (representing the British defending the fort) and 24 Boers (attacking the fort). Bell (1983) gives details of a game, *Asalto*, based on the Indian Mutiny (1857) in which three officers defend a fort attacked by fifty sepoys, the game being played on a board similar to that in Figure 4.15.

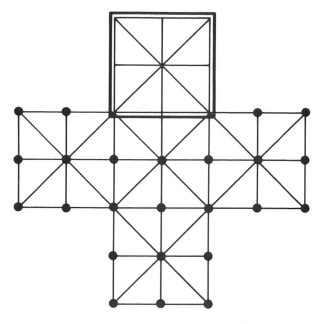

Figure *4.15*

Nineteenth century fairing 'The Chess Players' with minor damage to two chess pieces and one player's hand missing. (C 1870)

49

4.3 Investigations

Shaturanga

This game, like *Chess*, is a complex one to analyse but many of the 'standard' chessboard problems might be reconsidered. (Ball and Coxeter (1974) give interesting suggestions for chessboard investigations.)

  (i) What is the maximum number of Ships that can be placed on a chessboard so that no two are attacking each other? (Ships move two squares diagonally.)
 (ii) What is the least number of Ships that can be placed on a board so that, between them, they attack all the squares?

Lau Kati Kata

This is a reasonably 'simple' game to investigate before considering more complicated versions like *Sixteen Soldiers*. There are two possible opening moves for white; each move forces a particular response from black and then for white on the next move. The board then contains five white and five black pieces.

  (i) How many positions are possible after black has made a second move?
 (ii) Can two white pieces always force a win against one black piece?

The Maharajah and the Sepoys

  (i) Is there a 'best' initial position for the Maharajah? How many unoccupied squares does the Maharajah command when placed on each square?
 (ii) Consider the same problem for a chessboard containing no pieces other than the Maharajah.

Tablut

  (i) How many opening moves are possible for (*a*) the Swedes and (*b*) the Muscovites? Is there a 'best' opening move for each?
 (ii) What is the minimum number of moves in which each side could win? (Assume here that one of the players is an idiot!)

(iii) Consider the effect of changing the numbers in the two forces. (In an extreme case, if the King has no soldiers to defend and obstruct him, he wins!)

Fox and Geese

(i) What is the minimum number of geese needed to trap the fox?
(ii) If the geese start, what is the 'best' opening move? Why?
(iii) In how many ways could a single fox be placed on an empty board? Having placed the fox, in how many ways could a single goose be placed?
(iv) How many positions are possible with the fox and six geese left on the board? In how many of these is the fox trapped?
(v) Suggest a way in which a game might be recorded.

Lambs and Tigers

(i) In how many ways can a single tiger be placed on the board?
(ii) How many positions are possible with all the lambs and tigers on the board?
(iii) What is the minimum number of lambs needed to trap all three tigers?
(iv) What are the best places to put the lambs initially? Where should the tigers begin to move?
(v) Consider a simplified game on a smaller board with, say, one tiger and four or five lambs.

Cows and Leopards

(i) What are the best initial placements for the leopards?
(ii) What is the minimum number of cows needed for the cows to force a win?

Vultures and Crows

(i) How many crows must the vulture kill to make the crows too weak to trap him?
(ii) How many positions are possible with one vulture and one crow on the board?

(iii) How many positions are possible with all the pieces on the board?

The New Military Game of German Tactics

 (i) Investigate the 'best' initial placements for the officers. How many possible choices are there?
(ii) How many board positions are possible after one move by the men?
(iii) Invent a different 'military' game with a smaller board and fewer soldiers.

An earthenware figurine of two elderly gentlemen playing 'Siang K'i' (Chinese chess).

5 · Race games

5.0 Introduction

Race games appear to have been some of the earliest
games invented. They were used for divination – those
wishing to learn the future played against a priest, the
representative of the god whose advice was being sought.
Winning augured well but losing suggested a reappraisal
of plans which might range from proposed marriage to
declaration of war against a neighbour.

It is convenient to divide race games into three groups:

> The 'Backgammon' family
> Cross-and-circle games
> General race games.

Most race games involve the throw of a die or its
equivalent. Often cowrie shells or casting sticks are used.
A cowrie shell, when thrown, can land either mouth up
or mouth down and a casting stick (usually flat on one
side and rounded on the other) can fall flat side up or
down: thus both are equivalent to using coins and
throwing 'heads' or 'tails'. So, for example, in a game
using 4 casting sticks, there are **5** possible throws
corresponding to having 0, 1, 2, 3, or 4 flat sides
uppermost. The throwing of an object to determine a
move has always been an action open to suspicion of
cheating! Thus with a die some kind of cup is normally
used and with casting sticks it is common for them to be
thrown through a hoop or ring at a certain height above
the ground to ensure a fair throw.

5.1 The Backgammon family

The games described below are clear forerunners of
Backgammon, a game which has been described and
analysed in detail in many other places. (See, for
example, Waddington (1984) or Bell (1973).)

Tau

A painted plaster reproduction of an ancient Egyptian wall painting showing Queen Nefertari playing either 'Senat' or 'Tau'

The earliest boards in this group date from about 3000 BC and were discovered in the Royal Tombs of Ur in Iraq. The rules of some of the games are not known but the board in Figure 5.1a relates to a game called *Tau* ('robbers') played by the ancient Egyptians.

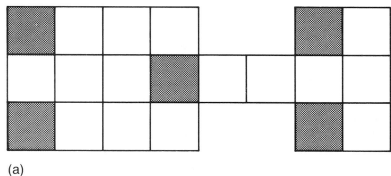

(a)

Figure 5.1(a)

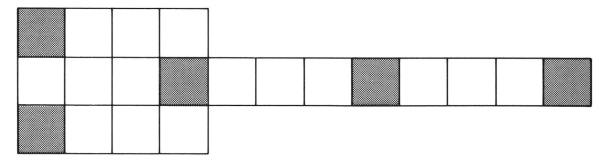

(b)

Figure 5.1(b)

Each board has 20 squares with some squares marked in a special way (either by colour or symbol). The board in Figure 5.1a was found in Ur and that in Figure 5.1b is thought to date from 1580 BC and was found in Cyprus. It is interesting to note that if the rectangle in board (a)

54

is extended into a single row, the two boards are in fact the same. The boards were discovered with casting sticks, made of black ebony on one side and white ivory on the other, used presumably to control the moves of pieces; or with dice shaped as tetrahedra with two vertices tipped in colour and two plain (thus they would be equivalent to coins or casting sticks). Also found were 20 carved pieces, ten lions and ten jackals. We are left to speculate on the rules of the game which was almost certainly a form of race in which the 'special' squares may have represented some form of 'safety' for pieces. It is interesting to note that if a player starts on any of the marked squares and only forwards/backwards or sideways moves are allowed (cf. Rook in *Chess*) then, by throwing a succession of fours, a piece could travel round the whole board landing only on the marked squares.

Senat

Another board from Egypt relates to a game called *Senat* (Figure 5.2). The earliest record of this game dates from a wall painting about 2650 BC. The symbol ⚷ denotes a 'gateway' or 'exit' and X, III, II, I represent 4, 3, 2, 1. The exact rules are not known but the following provides the basis for a possible game, assuming that all pieces follow the path indicated in Figure 5.3 (i.e. left to right – top row and bottom row; right to left – middle row).

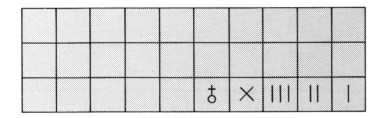

Figure 5.2

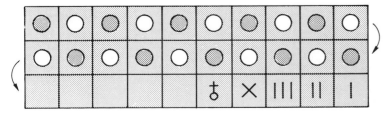

Figure 5.3

1. Each of two players has 10 pieces (black lions and white lions) and these are placed as shown in Figure 5.3.
2. Moves are made with a die which can show 1, 2, 3 or 4 (a 'long' die – see Figure 5.4).
3. A lion can be moved to an empty square or one containing an opponent's lion, in which case the enemy lion is captured and removed. A player cannot have more than one lion on a square.
4. Black starts. If the opening throw is 2, only the front lion can move. With a throw of 1, any enemy lion is captured. With a throw of 3, either the front lion is moved or an enemy lion is captured. With a throw of 4, one of the two front lions is moved.
5. Players play alternately and can move only forwards.
6. A lion reaching one of the squares X, III, II, I cannot be captured but rests there until an exact throw allows it to escape from the board (X = 4). A lion on ♂ is safe from attack but must move on as soon as possible. A piece must leave a marked square at the first possible opportunity.
7. The player who guides most lions safely off the board is the winner.

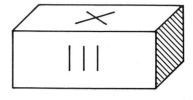

Figure 5.4

Tabula

Tabula was played by the Emperors Claudius (c. AD 50) and Zeno (c. AD 450), the former writing a book about the game and the latter becoming famous for a disastrous throw in a recorded game (see below). The board begins to resemble a modern *Backgammon* board (see Figure 5.5).

24	23	22	21	20	19	18	17	16	15	14	13
1	2	3	4	5	6	7	8	9	10	11	12

Figure 5.5

Each player has 15 pieces of a distinctive colour. All pieces enter the board at the same place and move in the same direction. Moves are controlled by three 6-sided dice. A throw of 3, 4, 5, for example, can be shared between pieces and could be used to move one piece by 12, or two pieces by 7 and 5 (or 8 and 4, or 9 and 3) or three pieces by 3, 4 and 5. If a player has two or more pieces on a square, the opponent cannot enter. If a player lands on a square occupied by a single opponent's piece, that piece is sent off the board and must reenter at the next possible throw. The winner is the first player to get all pieces off the board – an exact final throw is needed for each piece. Possible improvements to the game include: (i) no player is allowed to enter the second half of the board until all their pieces have been put into play; (ii) no piece is allowed to go off the end of the board until all a player's pieces are in the last quarter.

The famous, disastrous throw of Zeno took place with the position as in Figure 5.5. Zeno, playing white, threw 2, 5, 6 and was forced to unpile his pieces to leave eight single pieces (blots) vulnerable to removal by his opponent after being in a strong position. (This is assuming the rule that no pieces can go off the board until all a player's pieces are in the last quarter.)

Chasing the Girls

'Sugoroku' (Japanese Backgammon) board arranged for the game of 'Chase the Girls'

This game, still played in Iceland, is similar to *Tabula* and is usually played on a board on which the 'points' are thin wooden strips tacked onto a plank. The board is as in Figure 5.6.

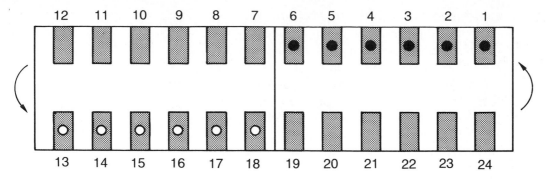

Figure 5.6

One player has 6 white 'girls' and the other 6 red. Figure 5.6 shows the opening position. Two dice are thrown but only throws of 6 or 1 or any double are used to move pieces anticlockwise round the board. A throw of a double gives a player an extra throw and a throw of 6, 6 enables a player to move four pieces 6 places each. If a piece lands on a point occupied by an opponent's piece, that piece is removed. Doubling up on a point is not allowed, and if a throw brings a player's piece to a point already occupied by one of their own pieces, the piece being moved is placed on the first vacant point beyond. Pieces continue to circulate around the board until one player has no pieces left.

When a player has only one piece left, it is known as a *corner-rattler* and lands only on the corner points of the four quarters of the board (points 1, 6, 7, 12, 13, 18, 19, 24); a throw of 1 moves it one corner point, 6 two corner points, and 1, 1 and 6, 6 count as double each of these throws – no other double counts. Thus, for example, if a corner-rattler is on 13 and the player throws 1, 6, the piece could move to 18 for the 1 and then to 24 (via 19) for the 6. Further a corner-rattler cannot be captured if it stands between enemy pieces. It is possible that both players will be reduced to corner-rattlers and then the game is likely to continue for a long time.

5.2 Cross-and-circle games

The early games in this group have a board which is made up of a cross and a circle. Later games often developed into either a cross or a circle alone.

Nyout

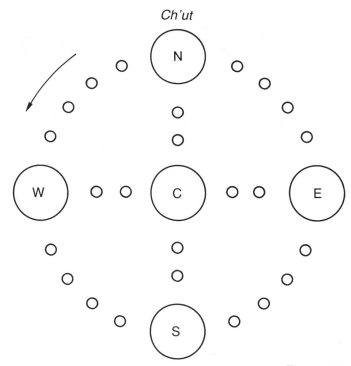

This game was played in Korea, probably before 1100 BC. The board (Figure 5.7) consists of 29 points made into a 'cross' and a 'circle'. The points at the horizontal and vertical extremes are larger than the others – the North is marked *Ch'ut* (Exit). The pieces used – usually made of stick or stone – are called *Mal* and they represent horses. They are moved using four dice known as *Pam-Nyout*. These 'dice' are pieces of stick about 2 cm long, flat and white on one side and convex and blackened by charring on the other. The rules are:

Figure 5.7

1. Two players have four horses each.
2. Each horse must start at N (counting the next point anticlockwise as the first) and finish at N (an exact throw is not necessary).
3. Throws of the sticks count as follows:

1 flat up	score 1
2 flats up	score 2
3 flats up	score 3
4 flats up	score 4
0 flats up	score 5

   If a score of 4 or 5 is achieved, the player has an extra throw; the scores are added together and can be used for one horse or split between two (or more) horses. (Thus, for example, a player might throw 5, 4, 2; the possible moves are then: one horse 11; two horses 9 and 2, or 7 and 4, or 5 and 6; or three horses 5, 4, and 2.)
4. If a horse lands on W, S or E, it must travel towards N through C. (Possible routes are NWCN, NSCN, NECN and N to N round the perimeter of the board.)

5. If a horse lands on another of the player's own horses, the two join together and move as one piece. Similarly three or four horses can join together.

6. If a piece lands on a point occupied by an opponent, the opponent is sent back to the start if the piece landing is made up of at least as many horses as the occupying piece. A piece cannot land on a point if the opponent already occupies that point with a piece of higher order.

Nyout is currently a popular gambling game in Korea, a similar game being recorded in the 3rd century AD. Cross-and-circle games found their way to North America, perhaps through immigrants from North East Asia; Figure 5.8 shows a Mayan game (c. AD 800) cut into a flagstone at Palenque.

The North American Indian games were often modified either by leaving out the cross and increasing the circle or by leaving out the circle and enlarging the cross.

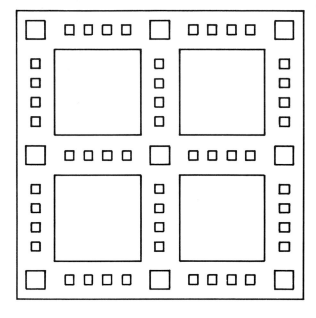

Figure 5.8

Ka-wa-su-suts

This is an example of a 'circle' game from New Mexico – the cross has disappeared. The board is marked out with 40 stones arranged in groups of 10 round a circle (see Figure 5.9) with four spaces or 'gates' called *Si-am-ma* placed North, South, East and West (these are the vestigial remains of a cross).

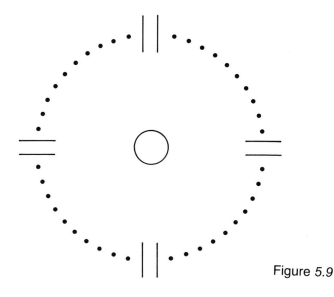

Figure 5.9

60

Players race round the circle as in *Nyout* and can go either clockwise or anticlockwise. Any of the gates is used as a starting point and moves are controlled by the throw of three sticks decorated with 2, 3 or 10 bands on one side and blank on the other. (Thus a player can score 0, 2, 3, 5, 10, 12, 13 or 15 as bands landing uppermost are counted.) A player moves a marker the appropriate number of spaces from the starting point after a throw. Players' pieces can be 'knocked off' by an opponent and made to start again – they are also returned to the start if they fall into one of the 'gates' which in some games are thought of as streams or gullies. Sometimes a round stone painted to represent a face and surrounded by a wreath of evergreens is placed to one side of the circle as a good luck talisman which is appealed to by the players before they make a throw. This stone is called *Kum-mushk-ko-yo* or 'Old Spider Woman'.

Patolli

Patolli is an Aztec game which is mentioned in an account written in the sixteenth century. It was played as a gambling game – before a game players would call on the god of gambling to favour their throws by sprinkling incense into a bowl of fire.

The game is played with six red and six blue stones; the dice are made up of five large black beans (*patolli*) with a hole drilled in one side to form a white 'pip'. Scoring is:

1 pip up	score 1
2 pips up	score 2
3 pips up	score 3
4 pips up	score 5
5 pips up	score 10

Figure 5.10

The board was a rush mat with a large cross painted on it (Figure 5.10). The original rules are unknown but the game involved a race round the outside of the board with pieces possibly travelling in both directions.

Pachisi

A cloth 'Pachisi' board with painted wooden pieces and cowrie shells from India. One player has made an opening move on a throw of four.

This game is a forerunner of *Ludo*. The double pathway in *Patolli* has become a triple one; as if, in a cross-and-circle game, the circle has become pressed against the arms of the cross with a large central square being left. *Pachisi* is widely played in India.

The board (Figure 5.11) is usually made of cloth. The marked squares are called 'castles' and on these a player

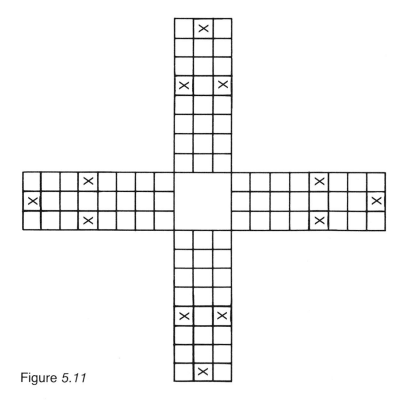

Figure *5.11*

is free from capture. The game is usually played by four players each having four pieces; those sitting opposite each other play as partners. Pieces are placed on the central square – the *char-koni* (throne) – at the start and they travel down their own limb, then anticlockwise round the board before returning to the middle via their limb. Moves are controlled by throws of six cowries – the number of mouths up determines the score for 2, 3, 4, 5 or 6, but 1 mouth up scores 10 and *no* mouths up scores 25. The basic rules are as follows:

1. A player's first piece can enter the board whatever the throw. Thereafter a piece can enter only with a throw of 6, 10 or 25.

2. A capture is made by a player landing on a square (other than a 'castle' square) occupied by an opponent's piece. The opponent's piece is returned to the centre and the player making the capture has another throw.

3. A player may refuse to play when it is his or her turn, or the player may throw and refuse to make use of the throw (this may be done to avoid risk of capture or to help the player's partner).

4. On reaching the 'castle' at the end of the third limb a player may wait there in safety until a 25 is thrown and then may move directly to the *char-koni*.

5. Pieces may double up on any square and move forward as a single piece. Doubled pieces can be sent back to start again if hit by an equal or larger number of opponent's pieces.

6. A piece cannot land on a 'castle' already occupied by an opponent's piece.

7. *Both* partners must get all pieces to the *char-koni* before the game ends. (Sometimes a leading player may wish to make a second circuit with a piece to help his or her partner.)

There are remains of courtyard *Pachisi* boards made of red and white marble squares at Agra and Allahabad palaces in Northern India. On these boards the emperor would play games using sixteen slaves from the harem, dressed in appropriate colours, as pieces – the use of children as pieces might produce an interesting school activity.

At about the end of the nineteenth century the game was modified by the introduction of a cubic die and the provision of separate starting points for each player, but the central square was retained and became 'home'. Thus the game of *Ludo* was born and introduced into England in 1896. There have been many variations produced, for example a game called *Broadway* appeared in America in 1917 based on a standard *Ludo* board but using locations such as Madison Square, Times Square, Seventh Avenue and Fifth Avenue as parts of the board. On a different theme a *Mickey Mouse Ludo* was marketed by the Chad Valley Company in Birmingham in the 1930s at a cost of two shillings and sixpence ($12\frac{1}{2}$ pence). Full details of both these variations are contained in Love (1979).

5.3   General race games

The Snake Game

This is an example of a spiral race game. It comes from Egypt and dates from before 3000 BC. The board is a coiled snake with the snake's head being at the centre and the body divided into a series of spaces varying from 29 to over 500. The drawing in Figure 5.12 is based on an illustration in Emery (1961).

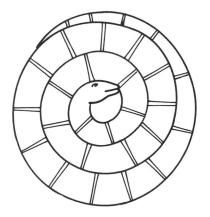

Figure *5.12*

   No exact rules are known but an illustration found in a tomb at Sakkara, dating from about 2700 BC, shows an equipment box containing six sets of six marbles with three lion and three hound figurines. Thus the game might have been for up to six players. If two players took part, each might have had six marbles and three animals and at each turn a player might try to guess the number of marbles held in the closed hand of the opponent – if the guess was right, the player would move that number of spaces, if wrong, the opponent would move. Such a system of scoring leads to interesting battles of wits between players! The idea of guessing a number held by an opponent is still common in games today; for example, a game called *Spoofing* enjoys popularity in inns in the West Country of England.

The Snail Game and other spiral games

Victorian England saw a proliferation of race games, among them being the *Snail Game* (which could have had its origin in the Egyptian *Snake Game*) appearing in about 1880. The board is merely a spiral in the form of a snail shell with 50 spaces. The following is a contemporary description taken from a booklet in a games compendium:

> This amusing game may be played by six or less, the more the merrier. Each player having thrown the dice, the highest starts the game, the next player on his left follows. The first player having thrown again shall place his marble the same number of holes forward. Should any player throw a number which carries his marble to an occupied hole, he must say 'You go back' and take his opponent's place. The player displaced must begin again. Any player throwing a higher number than required to reach the centre of game hole, must go back as many as the number thrown. Should that hole be occupied, then one further back.

There are many games which have been modelled on the original Egyptian idea of a snake. Two fascinating examples are included in Love (1979): *Pank-a-Squith* involves the suffragette leader Emmeline Pankhurst and her supporters encountering problems and obstacles as they race round a spiral track which leads to the House of Commons – the game was probably produced in 1909. Another spiral race occurs in *Round the World with Nellie Bly*, a game based on the adventures of Nellie Bly, an American journalist, who attempted to break the record created by Phineas Fogg in Jules Verne's *Around the World in Eighty Days* – the game dates from 1890. Thus many games throw interesting sidelights onto contemporary life and provide sociological and historical perspectives in addition to the playing and analysing which can always be done.

Snakes and Ladders and the Chinese Promotion Game

Snakes and Ladders is derived from an Indian divinitary game called *Moksha-patamu* used in religious education. According to the Hindu sages, virtuous acts (represented by ladders) shorten the journey of the soul through a number of incarnations to Nirvana, the state of ultimate perfection. Human sin, symbolised by the head of the snake, leads to reincarnation in a lower, animal form.

Thus *Snakes and Ladders* is a symbolic moral journey through life to heaven. Many variations have been produced (see Love, 1979); for example, *The Bonzo Chase*, which was produced for the British market in 1930, features Bonzo Dog (a popular cartoon character of the period).

A much older, similar type of game is the Chinese *Shing Kun t'o* (Promotion of the Mandarins) which was played at least as early as the Ming Dynasty (1368–1616). Four or more players took part, each having a piece whose moves recorded its owner's career. The board contained 98 spaces (see Figure 5:13) and the track ran round the board three times in a spiral and then up to the central square on which stood the imperial palace.

Entry onto the board was by the first 21 spaces; the remaining 77 spaces formed the track. Each space contained instructions for the next move and moves were controlled by six cubic dice. The value of a throw depended on the number of dice displaying the same number of pips:

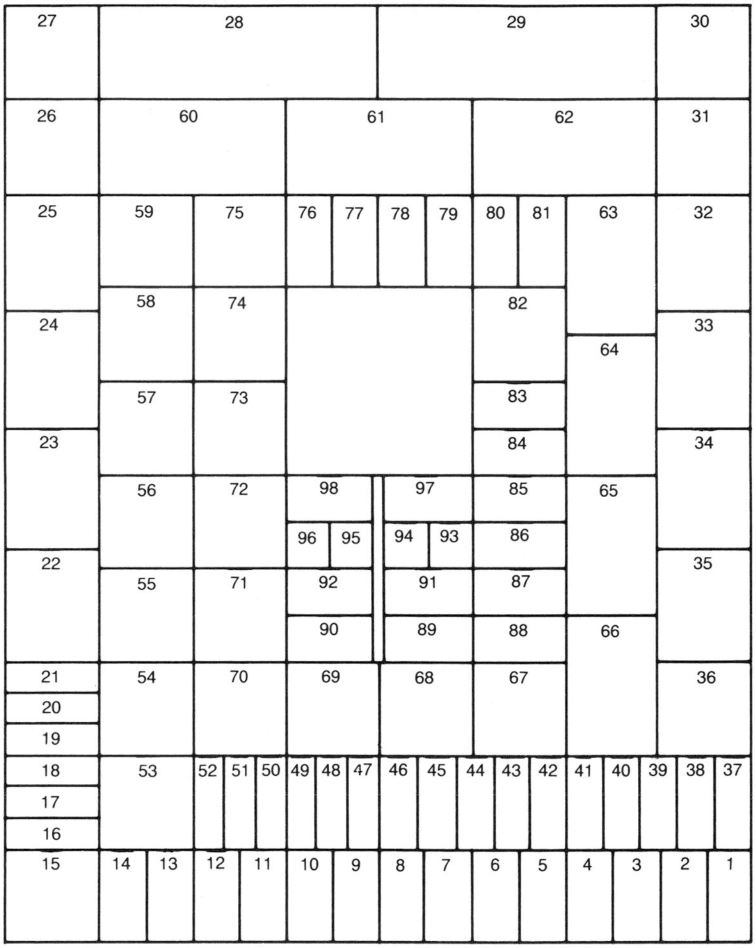

Figure 5.13

    throws of two alike entered pieces on squares 1 to 6
    throws of three alike entered pieces on spaces 9 to 14
    throws of four alike entered pieces on square 16 to 21
    throws of five alike entered pieces on square 7
    throws of six alike entered pieces on square 8 and
        gave another throw.

The idea has been copied many times. Games providing religious or moral instruction were popular in Victorian times. Examples appearing in Love (1979) include:

Cash, in which players race round a spiral trying to reach the central square and become millionaires. On the way qualities like honesty or attentiveness are rewarded whilst faults such as impudence or dullness are punished. The game comes from America and is late nineteenth century.

Office Boy and *District Messenger Boy*, dating from 1889 and 1896 respectively, both involve a spiral race to become head of the company and the person who is capable, earnest and ambitious is rewarded whilst the player who is careless, inattentive or dishonest is punished.

The Mansion of Happiness was invented by a clergyman's daughter and first published in 1843. It is subtitled 'An instructional, moral and entertaining amusement' and involves another spiral race, this time to the 'Mansion of Happiness'. The rules include: 'Whoever possesses Piety, Honesty, Temperance, Gratitude, Prudence, Truth, Chastity, Sincerity, Humility, Industry, Charity, Humanity or Generosity is entitled to advance six. Whoever possesses Audacity, Cruelty, Immodesty or Ingratitude must return to his former situation till his turn comes to throw again and not even think of Happiness, much less partake of it.'

A manufacturer's catalogue from the late nineteenth century observes, 'We have endeavoured with a conscientious regard for the good of the Youth of the land, to exclude from our list everything liable to abuse or tending to pervert the tastes of the old or Young.' There is a chapter entitled 'Games of Moral Improvement' in Whitehouse (1971). Similar games have been popular in recent years, for example, the *Game of Life* marketed by Milton Bradley Limited.

5.4 Investigations

Tau

(i) Given that a board is to have 20 squares and at least one line of symmetry, parallel to the sides of the squares, how many boards are possible? (It might be worth considering boards with smaller numbers of squares initially.)

(ii) Invent a board game based on the equipment found – for example, subsequent history suggests that pieces might be 'knocked off' on unmarked squares.

Senat

(i) Is it possible to have a game in which both players get all ten lions off the board? If so, what is the shortest sequence of moves to make this possible?

(ii) How many possible positions are there after two moves? How many after three moves?

(iii) Consider a board with a smaller number of lions or a smaller number of squares (or both). Discuss the questions asked above.

Tabula

(i) In how many ways can two dice be thrown? How many ways for three dice?

(ii) How many initial moves are possible for the first player (*a*) assuming two dice are used, (*b*) with three dice?

(iii) What would have been the best possible throw for Zeno?

(iv) Construct a simplified board consisting of two rows of six squares with each player having eight pieces. What is the least number of throws needed for the first player to win?

(v) What is the least number of throws needed for the first player to win on the actual *Tabula* board with 15 pieces?

Chasing the Girls

(i) How many positions are possible with all 12 pieces on the board?

(ii) Investigate a game played on a board with two rows of six points with players having three pieces each.

Nyout

(i) What is the quickest possible game?

(ii) Assuming no 'doubling up' of horses, what are the possible total lengths of routes for the four horses together? (Assume none are sent back.)

(iii) If you play on your own, how many sequences of throws are possible such that you cannot land any pieces on W?

(iv) Suppose the starting player throws 4, 5, 4, 5, 4, 2. How many choices are there? What is the 'best' move?

(v) Investigate the game on a smaller board and consider how the rules might need to be changed.

Ka-wa-su-suts

(i) What scores are possible on a throw?
(ii) How many sequences of throws land a player in the first 'gate'?
(iii) How many sequences land a player in the second 'gate'?

Pachisi

(i) Suppose a single player plays and moves four pieces round the board – what is the smallest number of throws needed to get all pieces home?
(ii) Investigate what would happen to a single piece starting from the centre if every throw was (a) 10, (b) 25.
(iii) Investigate similarities between the boards for *Tau* and *Pachisi*.

The Snake Game

Consider strategies for deciding how many marbles to hold and how many the second player should guess.

Chinese Promotion Game

(i) Consider possible patterns for a board, which must be a 'spiral', with 99 spaces.
(ii) In Figure 5.13, what is the maximum difference between the numbers in any two squares with a common boundary? Any point of intersection of lines in the figure is adjacent to several regions (for example, one such point in the centre is adjacent to 72, 73 and 98). For which point is the *total* of the numbers of these regions the greatest?
(iii) Investigate number patterns in Figure 5.13. For example, for chosen points, the sums of adjacent numbers are:

$95 + 96 + 98 = 289 = 17^2$
$97 + 93 + 86 + 85 = 361 = 19^2$
$53 + 54 + 19 + 18 = 144 = 12^2$

How many such perfect squares can be found?

6 · Dice, calculation and other games

6.0 Dice games: introduction

Dice are often used in board games, but there are also many games which use dice *alone*. Dicing was a favourite pastime in the Middle Ages and there is a reference by Ordericus Vitalis (1075–1143) who commented: 'Clergy and bishops are fond of dice playing'. In 1190 the yeomen-at-arms in the Crusaders under Richard the Lionheart of England and Philip of France were prohibited from playing any game for money, although knights and clergymen were allowed to play but subject to a fine of 100 shillings if they were found to have lost more than 20 shillings in one day. The two kings were exempt from all restrictions!

6.1 Games with two-sided dice

A coin forms a readily accessible two-sided die. Cowrie shells or sticks (rounded on one side and flat on the other) form 'dice' with two sides which do not have equal probabilities of falling one way or the other.

Pitch and Toss

This game was much played by miners in the first half of this century. Any number of players throw a penny towards a stick placed in the ground – the player who throws nearest the stick then throws the pennies in the air in turn calling 'heads' or 'tails' before they land. For each coin called correctly he or she wins a stake from each player, and winning pennies are withdrawn. The player who was second nearest the stick now plays with the remaining pennies, then the third nearest and so on.

Dittar Pradesh

This game, from Pakistan, uses sixteen cowrie shells. Any number of players each put a stake in a pool and then try to guess how many shells will fall mouth up at the next throw. The winning players (if any) share the pool.

Lu-Lu

Four round discs of volcanic stone about 2.5 cm in diameter are used in this game from Hawaii. The stones are plain on one side and marked as shown in Figure 6.1 on the other sides.

Players throw the stones in turn and count the number of dots scored – any stone falling with the plain side up is rethrown by the next player who adds any dots scored to their total. If a player throws 10 in one throw, they have another turn. The first player to reach an agreed score (say 100) is the winner.

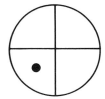 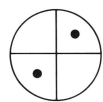 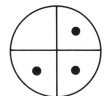 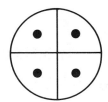

Figure 6.1

6.2 Games with four-sided dice

Ave Victrix

This game ('Hail Victor') has been put together from scattered references in classical writings. Four *astraguli* are used as dice (astraguli are small bones from the feet of mammals, usually sheep, and have been found in gaming material in Egyptian tombs and at Sumerian and Roman sites). Each bone has four surfaces which were named and had the following values:

Shape	Latin name	Translation	Score
Flat	Canis	Dog	1 point
Sinuous	Caesar	Prince	6 points
Concave	Volcanus	Vulcan	3 points
Convex	Aquila	Eagle	4 points

Any number of players play; they place a stake in a pool and cast the astraguli in turn. A game consists of ten rounds and the player with the highest score wins the pool at the end. There are several special throws:

- if all four faces are different, the caster wins the pool immediately;
- if four dogs are thrown the player retires from the game;
- four vulcans, eagles or princes score four times the face value of the throw and a bonus of 20 points;
- a throw of three of any kind carries a bonus of 10 points;
- a throw of two pairs carries a bonus of 5 points.

Sheep's astraguli for 'Ave Victrix'. From left to right: Volcanus 3 (concave); Aquila 4 (convex); Canis 1 (flat); Caesar 6 (sinuous). In front is a Roman astragal of lead from the third century AD, found in Lincolnshire.

6.3 Games with cubic dice

Four—Five—Six

A tourist's souvenir from Reno, Nevada. Note the dice on the stool.

This is a game from the American Far West in which three cubic dice are thrown. Each player places a wager on the table and a 'banker' plays against each player in turn. When the banker or a player throws 4, 5, 6, or any pair and a 6, or three of a kind, it is a *winning* combination. However, throws of 1, 2, 3, or any pair and a 1, are *losing* combinations. If any pair is thrown with a 2, 3, 4 or 5 this is called throwing a *point*. Then if the opponent fails to score a winning or losing combination but throws a point the player with the higher single number wins. If a player throws any other throw, they must throw again until a win or a loss or a point is thrown. The banker always throws first (so that, for example, if 4, 5, 6 is thrown, the banker wins without the other player having a throw).

Poker Dice

Pupils playing 'Poker Dice'. The board and leather dice cup are Mexican and are decorated with Aztec sun discs.

Five special dice are used for this game with faces marked Ace (A), King (K), Queen (Q), Jack (J), Ten (T) and Nine (N). The object is to throw the highest poker hand in either one or two throws as decided by the player – after the first throw the player may keep what they have or rethrow one, two or three dice. The order of scoring (lowest to highest) is:

> Pair
> Two pairs
> Three of a kind
> Full house (three of a kind and a pair)
> Four of a kind
> Low flush (a sequence N, T, J, Q, K)
> Royal flush (a sequence T, J, Q, K, A)
> Five of a kind

Sequences

Players throw six dice. A throw containing three 1's cancels a player's whole score. Otherwise scores are achieved for throws as follows:

Throw containing	Score
1, 2	5
1, 2, 3	10
1, 2, 3, 4	15
1, 2, 3, 4, 5	20
1, 2, 3, 4, 5, 6	25

The first to score 100 points is the winner.

6.4 Calculation games

Rithmomachia

The earliest record of this game, for two players, appears in an eleventh-century manuscript. *Rithmomachia* seems to have been popular with intellectuals in the Middle Ages, being regarded by some as superior to *Chess*. It is played on a board with 144 squares (8 × 16) set up as shown in Figure 6.2.

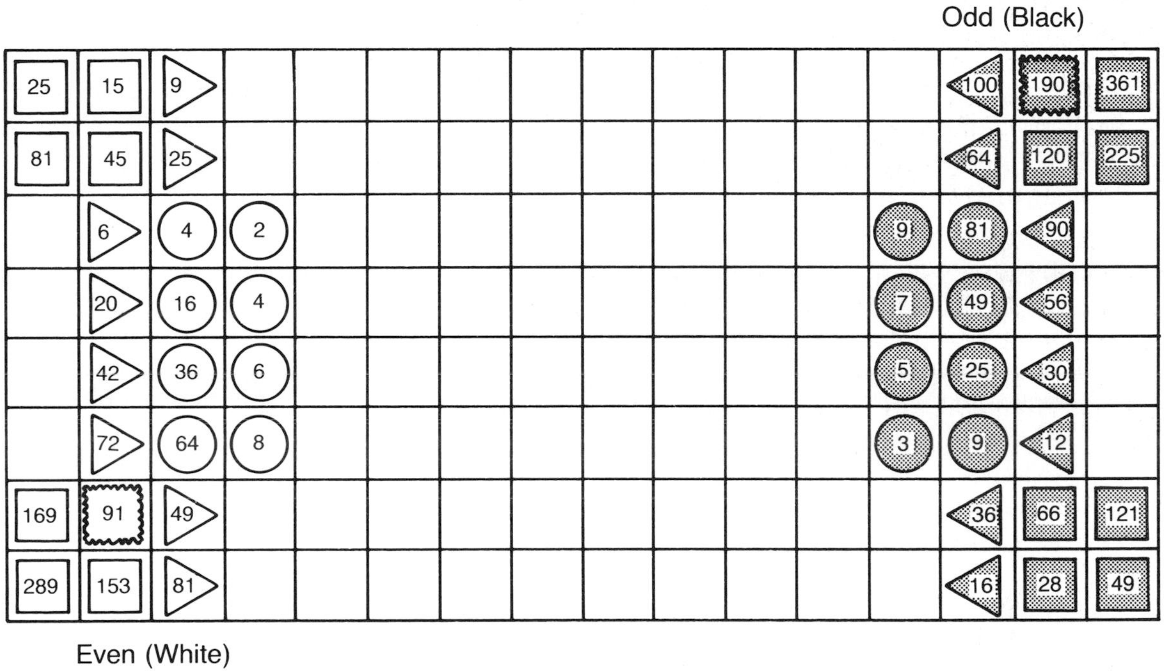

Odd (Black)

Even (White)

Figure 6.2

Each player has pieces in the form of 'rounds', 'triangles', 'squares' and a 'pyramid'. One player has white pieces (or 'evens') and the other black (or 'odds'). The pyramids are made up of separate pieces: rounds, triangles and squares – for white,

$$91 = 1 + 4 + 9 + 16 + 25 + 36$$

(i.e. two rounds, two triangles and two squares); for black,

$$190 = 16 + 25 + 36 + 49 + 64$$

(i.e. one round, two triangles and two squares).

Players move alternately and move one piece at a time:

- a *round* can move to any adjacent empty space.
- a *triangle* can move three empty spaces in any direction.
- a *square* can move four empty spaces in any direction.
- a *pyramid* can move the same way as any of its layers.

The object of the game is to capture opponent's pieces in some desired combination. Captures are made in four ways:

(i) by landing on an occupied square;

(ii) by moving to a position such that the number of the piece multiplied by the number of vacant squares between this piece and an opponent's piece is equal to the number of the opponent's piece (for example, if white's '4' is separated by nine vacant squares from black's '36');

(iii) by moving pieces to either side of an opponent's piece such that the sum of the pieces is equal to the opponent's number (for example, white would capture black's '12' by sandwiching it between '4' and '8');

(iv) by surrounding a piece on four sides.

There are several ways of winning and players decide in advance on the kind of game to be played. *Common Victories* (games suitable for beginners) include:

(i) agreement on a number of pieces to be captured for a win (e.g. 15);

(ii) agreement on the *total value* of pieces to be captured (e.g. 160);

(iii) as in (ii) but with the number of digits in the captured pieces specified, e.g. a total of 160 and eight digits when 56, 64, 28 and 12 would be a winning series of captures;

(iv) as in (ii) but also with a specified number of pieces, e.g. 150 and five pieces when 100, 28, 12, 7 and 3 would win;

(v) a combination of (ii), (iii) and (iv) so that victory might need a total of 160, five pieces and ten digits.

Proper Victories (games suitable for advanced players) involve achieving arithmetic, geometric and harmonic progressions using pieces which must include one captured from the opponent. [Note: an *arithmetic progression* is a sequence in which any term is a fixed amount more (or less) than the previous term e.g. 3, 6, 9, 12, . . . A *geometric progression* has any term a fixed multiple of the previous term e.g. 2, 4, 8, 16, . . . A *harmonic progression* is a sequence such that the reciprocals of the terms are in arithmetic progression, e.g. 3, 4, 6, 12, . . .]

There are three levels for a proper victory:

(i) having three pieces which form one of the three progressions to win (e.g. 2, 3, 4 as an arithmetic progression, 4, 6, 9 as a geometric progression, or 2, 3, 6 as a harmonic progression);

(ii) having four pieces which form *two* different progressions (e.g. 2, 3, 4, 6 giving an arithmetic and a harmonic progression);

(iii) having four pieces which form *three* different progressions (e.g. 4, 6, 9, 12 giving 6, 9, 12 – arithmetic; 4, 6, 9 – geometric; and 4, 6, 12 – harmonic).

Players may wish to modify the rules before playing – actual numbers might be changed, the number of pieces and/or the size of the board might be varied. However, the game lends itself to endless possibilities for number work and investigation; some suggestions are made at the end of the chapter.

6.5   Other games

Pegs in Holes

This is a solitaire game which has its origins in chessboard problems, see for example Ball and Coxeter (1974). The board (Figure 6.3) consists of six rows of six holes and the player has six pegs. These pegs must be placed in holes so that no two pegs are connected by a straight line.

The game was sold in London for one penny (old) at the end of the last century.

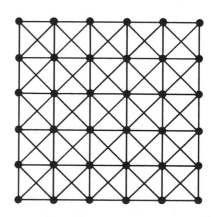

Figure 6.3

Officers and Nationalities

This is another solitaire game, using the board in Figure 6.4, in which a player has 36 pieces. The pieces represent soldiers with the ranks Lieutenant, Captain, Major, Colonel, Brigadier and General. There is one officer of each rank from each of the countries Belgium, England, France, Ireland, Scotland and Wales. On a 6 × 6 board with 36 squares, the pieces must be arranged so that no row or column contains soldiers of the same rank or the same nationality.

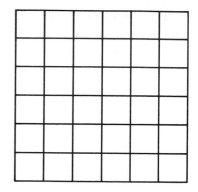

Figure 6.4

A variation on this game has a board of 100 squares (10 × 10) and soldiers of 10 different ranks from 10 different countries must be similarly arranged.

This game is based on a problem suggested by the mathematician Euler in 1782.

Kirkman's Schoolgirls

Thomas Kirkman was a clergyman from Cheshire who first suggested the following problem in 1847:

> Fifteen young ladies in a school walk out three abreast for seven days in succession: it is required to arrange them daily so that no two will walk twice abreast.

Thus the problem is to arrange the 15 girls in five groups of three in seven ways so that no pair ever appears together. A simple 'game' can be developed from this problem by using 105 counters, seven each numbered 1, 2, . . . , 15; the counters then need to be arranged in the way suggested by the problem. It is interesting to note that the original problem has been linked with discussion of unwanted crackle on telephone lines and with 'balanced incomplete block designs' in recent years (see Cartwright (1986)).

Noro

The *New Royal Game of Noro* probably dates from the early part of this century. It is played on the board shown in Figure 6.5.

One player has five counters numbered 1, 2, 3, 4, 5 and puts these irregularly on the *coloured* spaces – the other player has five counters coloured brown, yellow, green, red and blue and puts them irregularly on the *numbered* spaces. Players then move alternately. They may move a counter one spot at a time along a line to an empty adjacent spot (backwards, forwards or sideways). The winner is the first player to get all their counters on the correct spots.

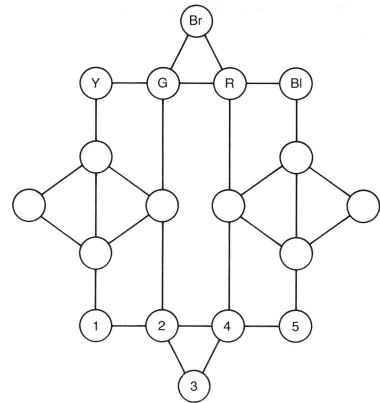

Figure 6.5

Marvellous '26'

This game, for one player, was sold by T. Ordish in London for sixpence (2$\frac{1}{2}$p) probably in about 1920. The board is as in Figure 6.6 and the player has twelve discs numbered 1 to 12.

The discs must be arranged to make the greatest number of runs totalling 26, either in straight lines, angles or other geometric figures. The makers of the game, on the box in which it was sold, comment:

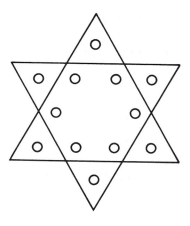

Figure 6.6

> A child could probably make from one to three or four 'twenty sixes' along the sides of the two triangles but the more advanced operator may make each of the six sides as well as the six spaces round the centre total up to 26 with perhaps the finding of several additional 'twenty sixes'. Thus the worker is rewarded or encouraged while in an ordinary puzzle there is entire failure short of entire success.

The final sentence here provides interesting comment on possible philosophies of problem solving!

6.6 Investigations

Pitch and Toss

(i) If there are three players, what is the probability that the game finishes before the last player has a turn?

(ii) What is the probability that the last player has three pennies to throw?

(iii) How many possible outcomes are possible after the first two players have thrown?

(iv) Consider the game with 4, 5, . . . players.

Dittar Pradesh

If three players call 5, 6, 7 respectively, and the probability of a shell landing mouth up is $1/3$, what is the probability that the pool is won?

Lu-Lu

(i) What scores are possible in two throws of the stones and in how many ways can they be achieved?

(ii) Assuming no 'extra' throws (from stones falling with a plain side up and being passed on), in how many ways can 50 be reached in exactly six throws?

(iii) Consider a simpler game with three stones marked with 1, 2 and 3 dots. Also a harder game with five stones marked 1 to 5.

Ave Victrix

(i) What scores are possible in a single turn?

(ii) Can a player score *exactly* 1000 in ten throws?

Four—Five—Six

(i) What is the probability that the game is won or lost by the banker without the other player throwing?

(ii) Invent, and investigate, a similar game with (*a*) two dice and (*b*) four dice.

A Chinese filigree ivory dicing cup decorated with mythical dragons (C1890) and modern chinese dice.

Poker Dice

(i) How many initial throws are possible?
(ii) If you throw J, J, J, K, K, what is the probability of improving on this throw by rethrowing (a) K, K

(b) J, J, J?

Sequences

How many throws scoring nothing are possible?

Rithmomachia

Of all the games in this book this one has the largest range of possibilities for number investigations.

(i) How are the numbers on the board derived? (Hint: can the values of all the pieces be expressed in terms of the front lines, viz. 2, 4, 6, 8 and 3, 5, 7, 9?)
(ii) In how many ways could 160 be made up from each player's pieces? What other numbers would make suitable targets?

(iii) With the numbers on the board, how many sets of three form arithmetic, geometric or harmonic progressions? (Can a set of three numbers be more than one of these progressions at the same time?)
(iv) How many sets of four form two of the three types of progressions? How many sets of four form all three types?
(v) Consider *all* integers (not just those on the board). Find all possible sets of four integers which contain all three progressions.

Pegs in Holes

Find a solution to the problem. Investigate for boards with different numbers of holes – clearly no solution would be possible on a 2 × 2 board, but what about other sizes?

Officers and Nationalities

Look for solutions for the problems with 36 and 100 soldiers. What happens with 4, 9, 16, 25, . . . soldiers?

Kirkman's Schoolgirls

Solve the problem. Investigate also 9 girls walking on 4 days, 21 girls walking on 10 days, for example.

Noro

What is the least number of moves needed for a player to win?

Marvellous '26'

(i) Find possible combinations of 1, 2, . . . , 12 which add up to 26.
(ii) Arrange the numbers so that all six sides of the triangles make a '26' – also make the numbers round the central hexagon add up to 26.
(iii) The makers claim it is possible to show more than 30 runs of '26' in one arrangement. Is this possible?

7 . Games and investigations in the classroom

7.0 General comments

Children are nowadays expected to pursue more and more 'investigations' in mathematics, increasingly for purposes of assessment. Undoubtedly it is possible to provide pupils with training and practice so that they are able to become experienced in carrying out investigational work but ultimately an individual's level of motivation and interest is crucial. This chapter contains details of work carried out by children when some of the suggestions for investigations made in this book and based on the games described were tried in schools. Most work was done with pupils between the ages of ten and seventeen – sometimes with children in groups as large as 35, sometimes with individuals and sometimes with small groups working as teams.

Observations of pupils attempting to carry out suggested tasks have led to the following broad conclusions and generalisations (although they are, of course, not universally true!).

(i) Pupils generally need both clear guidance and concrete materials so that they can actually *play* a game and handle boards and pieces when investigating (this comment does no more than endorse the work of psychologists like Piaget and Dienes).

(ii) Without practice and/or careful direction, children find it difficult to produce a written account of work done. Two extremes are represented by (*a*) the pupil who is unable to edit or select and who produces a long, incomprehensible write-up including *everything* done and (*b*) the pupil who destroys *all* work except for a brief summary of conclusions.

In the process of writing, *notation* is *crucial* and part of the task (for most pupils) lies in the development of a suitable method to use to record a game or to use in its analysis. Polya (1957) writes, 'An important step in solving a problem is to choose the notation. It should be done carefully . . . choosing a suitable notation may contribute essentially to understanding the problem.'

(iii) Although an investigation provides a good *individual* exercise, pupils gain much through exchange of ideas with others, especially in the early stages of a piece of work.

(iv) Rarely does a single investigation given to a large group produce consistently good work.

(v) A vague suggestion that something might be investigated does not often yield good results whereas carefully selected, specific suggestions will frequently get pupils started and they will subsequently find other avenues to explore without further guidance. For example, an approach which begins with the question: 'Investigate the game of *Tablut*' is likely to be less successful than one which asks: (*a*) How many opening moves are there in *Tablut*? (*b*) How many positions are possible after two moves? (*c*) Investigate possible openings. (*d*) Invent a simplified version of the game. And so on.

Pupils tended to show higher levels of interest when some background material dealing with, for example, superstitions pertaining to a game, its history, its geographical background, or possible variations were introduced.

In the investigation of games, it is surprising how often the same piece of mathematics can appear in a number of different places. In mathematics itself there are many examples of the same basic structure existing in different parts of the subject (e.g. 'group' structure will appear – at least implicitly – in the geometry of transformations, in modulo arithmetic and in work on numbers and number bases). Throughout this book there are many themes which appear repeatedly. As an example of one such theme consider the number of ways of placing p things in n holes – this problem occurs:

(i) In the game *Mankal'ah Al-Ghashim* (Chapter 3); 'If you have a twelve-hole mancala board and must place 72 seeds in the twelve holes with at least four in each hole, how many arrangements are possible?' i.e. the problem is to place 24 things in twelve holes.

(ii) In *Nyout* (Chapter 5): 'If four horses get home by travelling either 11, 16, 20 or 21 squares, in how many ways can they all get home?' i.e. in how many ways can four 'things' be put in four 'holes'?

(iii) In *Tabula* (Chapter 5): 'In how many ways can three dice be thrown?' i.e. how many ways of placing three 'things' in six 'holes'?

These three examples all provide instances of the use of the general result that p things can be placed in n holes in $^{n+p-1}C_{n-1}$ ways. Thus as well as games providing scope for individual analysis, there is also undoubtedly ample opportunity for examination of links between different games.

7.1 Investigations into games of position

Pong Hau K'i

The advantage of this game (see Section 2.3) is that it is very simple indeed and can therefore be tried with young children. Indeed the simplicity often led pupils to think that there was really nothing to investigate! Most children found the game initially attractive and soon found that a draw could always be achieved. There was difficulty in finding a clear, concise way in which to represent moves and often a desire to force a conclusion (e.g. 'the second player always wins') when none existed. Figure 7.1 shows some attempts by twelve-year-olds at recording games played.

The activity induced by the game was more successful when specific suggestions were made. For example, how many positions are possible after two moves? How many positions are possible altogether?

One teacher who tried the game with a group of eight- and nine-year-old children reported: 'everyone seemed to enjoy it immensely. One boy returned to the classroom in his spare time to make a copy of it. I found there was great interest and excitement and children were keen to organise their own class competition. I was interested to see how children responded socially.'

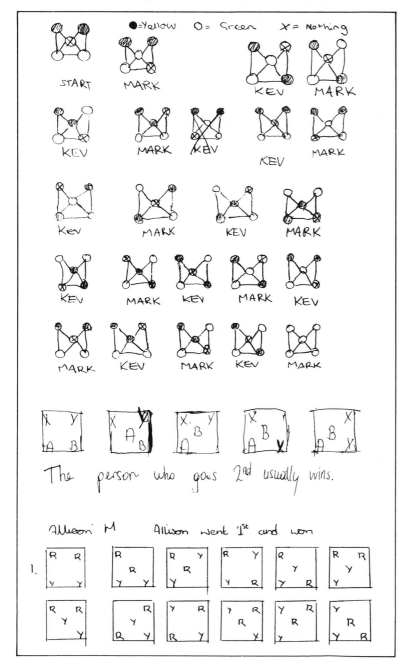

Figure 7.1

Three Men's Morris

Three Men's Morris (or *Nine Holes*) – see Section 2.1 – was tried with a class of twelve-year-old pupils. The game led to some clumsy attempts to produce a notation for recording as shown in Figure 7.2. However, the game was successful as a sophisticated form of *Noughts and Crosses*. Although some children began to attempt to analyse early positions in the game, most did not go far beyond speculation about whether the first or second player should win. Similar work on the game of *Seega* (Section 2.1) tried with a group of eleven-year-olds led to much discussion on the counting (or not counting) of reflections of the board as being different positions.

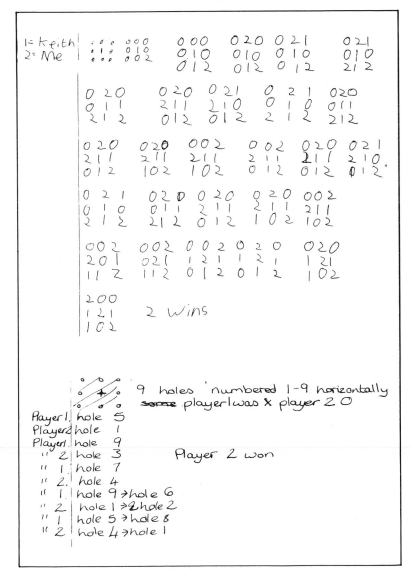

Figure 7.2 *Three Men's Morris* recorded by twelve-year-olds

7.2 Mancala investigations

'Egg Box' Mancala

The investigations described in Chapter 3 were tried with a wide variety of different groups mainly between the ages of eleven and fourteen. Without guidance, very few pupils at the bottom end of this age range were able to

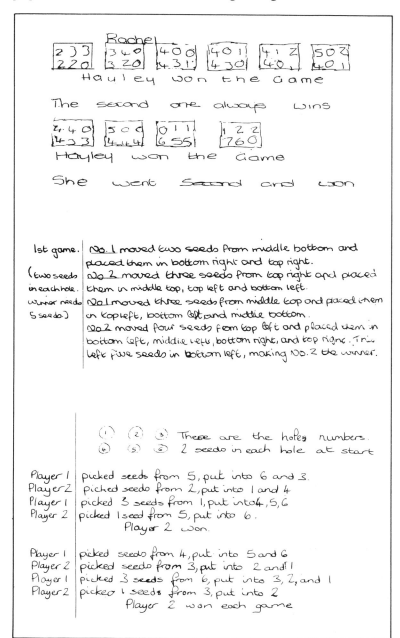

Rachel

| 2 3 3 | 3 4 0 | 4 0 0 | 4 0 1 | 4 1 2 | 5 0 2 |
| 2 2 0 | 3 2 0 | 4 3 1 | 4 3 0 | 4 0 2 | 4 0 1 |

Hayley won the Game

The second one always wins

| 2 4 0 | 5 0 0 | 0 1 1 | 1 2 2 |
| 4 2 3 | 4 4 4 | 6 5 5 | 7 6 0 |

Hayley won the Game

She went Second and won

1st game.   No. 1 moved two seeds from middle bottom and placed them in bottom right and top right.

(Two seeds in each hole.   No. 2 moved three seeds from top right and placed them in middle top, top left and bottom left.

winner needs   No. 1 moved three seeds from middle top and placed them 5 seeds.)   in top left, bottom left and middle bottom.

No. 2 moved four seeds from top left and placed them in bottom left, middle left, bottom right, and top right. This left five seeds in bottom left, making No. 2 the winner.

---

① ② ③ These are the holes numbers.
④ ⑤ ⑥ 2 seeds in each hole at start

Player 1	picked seeds from 5, put into 6 and 3.
Player 2	picked seeds from 2, put into 1 and 4.
Player 1	picked 3 seeds from 1, put into 4, 5, 6
Player 2	picked 1 seed from 5, put into 6.
	Player 2 won.

Player 1	picked seeds from 4, put into 5 and 6
Player 2	picked seeds from 3, put into 2 and 1
Player 1	picked 3 seeds from 6, put into 3, 2, and 1
Player 2	picked 1 seeds from 3, put into 2
	Player 2 won each game

Figure 7.3 'Egg Box' Mancala recorded by twelve-year-olds

record games in a concise way. The investigations in Section 3.4 were tried using egg boxes and counters. Children would often draw a complete 'board' repeatedly in their recording of the game or write a long account rather than try to introduce any notation – some examples are given in Figure 7.3.

There was little attempt to justify any conclusions and comments like 'the player who starts should win' were often made without further comment and based usually on a small sample of actual games.

Tchuka Ruma

This game (Section 3.3) proved immensely popular with all ages, perhaps because there was a very clear *aim* to the investigation and a satisfying outcome when the initial problem was solved. The majority of pupils applied a 'trial and error' approach, few worked systematically and few attempted to show that the solution to the game is unique. Some above-average pupils in the thirteen–fourteen age range looked at variations – some of these are shown in Figure 7.4.

It is interesting to note that, when *Tchuka Ruma* was given to a group of 20 sixth-formers, nearly all reacted by producing practical material (coins, torn-up pieces of paper etc.) to act as pieces and none showed the confidence to tackle the problem solely with pencil and paper. One teacher with a mixed-ability class of twelve-year-olds introduced the game as a 'people' game using chairs to represent holes with pairs of children to represent pebbles – the children then dispersed to tackle the game using counters and were encouraged to record their moves. Some comments on *Tchuka Ruma* from this group appear in Figure 7.5.

The teacher commented on one pupil:

> Dawn, although not noted for her mathematical prowess, saw no difficulty and was happy to demonstrate to her neighbours. In subsequent investigational work she regularly demonstrated a logical, well-organised approach which amazed and impressed me and caused me to reassess her mathematical ability.

We played the game to the original rules and found that if you start at hole 3, and follow the moves listed below, the game can be completed.

START				
2	2	2	2	0
2	2	0	3	1
3	3	0	0	2
3	0	1	1	3
3	0	0	2	3
4	0	0	0	4
0	1	1	1	5
0	1	1	0	6
0	0	2	0	6
0	0	0	1	7
0	0	0	0	8

Another theory.

We thought that if the $\dfrac{\text{number of counters}}{\text{number of holes}}$ equaled $\dfrac{1}{2}$, the game would be completed. This was proved wrong because $\dfrac{1 \text{ counter}}{2 \text{ holes}} = \dfrac{1}{2}$ but the game cannot be completed. The game which can be completed is $\dfrac{1 \text{ counter}}{3 \text{ holes}}$ which equals $\dfrac{1}{3}$ and does not fit the theory.

Other ideas that could be tried in the process of investigating Tchuka Ruma are-

a) Use varied amounts of counters in a set number of holes. i.e ① ② ③ ④ Ⓡ
 1   4   2   2   0 and then see what happens. if you can work it out or if there are any patterns you can notice.

b) Try to find out why, if you change the position of the Ruma, do you always end up putting your last coin at the end (where the original Ruma was)? Why won't it work? Are there any patterns similar to the 1st arrangement

c) What happens if you use more than one Ruma?

Figure 7.4 *Tchuka Ruma* suggestions from fourteen-year-olds

I thought it was hard and only a clever pupil could do it.

It Drived us Nutty. Its frustrating.

What gets us stuck is putting a counter is good. It is very the game itself empty hole. But confusing.

I think it is good but after a while it gets boaring because you forget how to do it and I could not do it at all.

I thought this game was easy but enjoyable.

It was good, hard until you found out the way to do it. After a bit if you never got it right I think you would just give up

It was complecated

Figure 7.5   Comments on *Tchuka Ruma*

91

7.3 War games

Tablut

This proved a popular game to play but there was often difficulty in getting any detailed 'investigation' from pupils. Attempts to vary the numbers of pieces on each side produced uneven contests and games on smaller boards often became trivial. A number of different notations for recording the game were produced, the most obvious and successful being a 'coordinate' system with squares numbered 1–9 on one side and labelled R–Z on another. Thus one game produced:

Muscovites	Swedes
U9–S9	V4–X4
S5–S1	V5–V4
S9–S2	V4–W4
V2–Y2	W4–S4
V9–S9	S4–S8
R6–R8	V7–R7
V8–T8	S8–S7
Z6–Z7	X5–X9
W9–W7	S7–V7
S9–V9	V7–V8
Y5–Y8	V8–V7
T8–W8	X9–X7
S2–S9	V7–S7
Y2–Y7	V3–R3
U1–U2	S7–S2

and the Swedes win as their King has reached the edge of the board.

As a game to play and as a vehicle for recording via coordinates, *Tablut* was successful. As a stimulus for further work it was (perhaps surprisingly) less successful. With *Tablut*, as with many of the games in this book, children were eager to produce their own 'similar' games – a modern game called *Pente* (manufactured by the Palitoy Company) which involves a combination of a 'five-in-a-row' game of position and the 'custodian' method of capture of *Tablut*, was one such game to be produced.

Fox and Geese and other animal games

Reactions to these games varied. At one extreme the suggested lines of investigation proved too easy and at the other problems posed proved to be almost impossible to solve! Thus, for example, in *Fox and Geese* (see Section 4.2) most pupils had little trouble in determining the minimum number of geese needed to trap the fox but there was much confusion in trying to establish how many positions were possible with a fox and six geese left on the board – here there was (inevitably?) a problem in trying to cope with reflections and rotations of the board. These problems did at least produce some interesting work and discussion on the nature of reflections and rotations.

7.4   Race games

Two unexpected (and exciting) pieces of work emerged from games in this section.

Senat

This game (Section 5.1) was presented as a 'mystery' – the board and pieces had been discovered but no rules were known. Such an approach led to much conjecture and some highly original thought and suggestions. Using the rules suggested in Chapter 5, one question asked was, 'How many possible positions are there after two moves?' This question prompted one pupil (aged twelve) to produce the work shown in Figure 7.6:

The patterns

    90, 18, 90, 26   10, 1, 10, 2
    91, 18, 91, 26   20, 2, 20, 4

then provoked further investigation. The fourth group is double the second group and the third group is almost the same as the first. Is there any relationship? Unprompted, the pupil then tried a *Senat* board with five (instead of ten) pieces of each colour and came up with the patterns:

    20, 8, 20, 11   5, 1, 5, 2
    21, 8, 21, 11   10, 2, 10, 4

and again a similar relationship between groups seems
to exist.

Although this particular pupil was unable to reach any
definite generalisation without help, the initial thinking
provided some superb opportunities for pattern spotting
and the eventual realisation that the pattern was:

$$n(n-1), \quad 2(n-1), \quad n(n-1), \quad 3n-4 \qquad n, \quad 1, \quad n, \quad 2$$
$$n^2-n+1, \quad 2(n-1), \quad n^2-n+1, \quad 3n-4 \qquad 2n, \quad 2, \quad 2n, \quad 4$$

and that these numbers give a sum: $4n^2 + 12n - 1$

Throws		Positions	
1	1	90	
1	2	18	①
1	3	90	
1	4	26	
2	1	10	
2	2	1	②
2	3	10	
2	4	2	
3	1	91	
3	2	18	
3	3	91	③
3	4	26	
4	1	20	
4	2	2	
4	3	20	④
4	4	4	

Total = 519

The numbers in ④ are twice those in ②.
It is nearly true that ① and ③ are the same.

Figure 7.6   A pupil's work
on *Senat*

Nyout

The innocent-looking question which asked 'What are the possible total lengths of routes for four horses?' prompted work along the following lines:

Routes possible are 11, 16, 20, and 21 spaces. Thus we must pick four of these numbers with repetitions being allowed.

The problem is now that of having four (large) piles of sweets from which we can choose any four sweets.

The pattern now produced was:

We can choose 1 sweet in 4 ways
2 sweets in 10 ways
3 sweets in 20 ways
4 sweets in 35 ways (the answer to the question)
5 sweets in 56 ways
6 sweets in 84 ways

. . . this was as far as a twelve-year-old pupil got.

There is a nice 'sixth-form' investigation here. In general we can choose p things from 4 piles in

$$^{p+3}C_3 = (p + 3)(p + 2)(p + 1)/3! \text{ ways}$$

or p things from n piles in

$$^{n+p-1}C_{n-1} \text{ ways.}$$

7.5 Dice, calculation and other games

Rithmomachia

Trying to play this game produced much complication and confusion until clear rules were established. The 'code' of the original board was solved in a variety of ways – at a low level there was often some difficulty in the algebraic expression of some of the numbers on the pieces.

The search for sets of numbers which exhibited arithmetic, geometric and harmonic progressions led to:

(i) a pupil writing a simple computer program to test sets of four numbers for arithmetic, geometric and harmonic progressions and 'discovering' the only three sets of four numbers to contain all three progressions.

(ii) pupils tryings to establish by an algebraic argument the conditions needed for a set of four numbers:

$$a \quad b \quad c \quad d$$

to contain triples in each of the three types of progression.

(iii) the 'discovery', by young pupils, that, in choosing a number of things from a larger number, the pattern formed is that of Pascal's triangle.

There is unlimited scope here for the creation of other calculation games and pupils showed great imagination and cunning in the invention of such games.

Dice games

Dice games seemed to hold a particular attraction. From the teacher's point of view they provide a set of games which need only very simple equipment.

It was interesting to observe that pupils would carry out some quite complex analyses when given tasks which were based on a game but that they would be less willing and less interested to carry out the same tasks in isolation. Thus, for example, great enthusiasm was shown in working out the number of ways in which three dice could be thrown to start a game of *Tabula* (see Section 5.1) whilst the task of working out the number of ways as a separate activity was tackled with much greater reluctance. (Perhaps we are noting here the simple fact that mathematics which relates to something 'real' is much more readily tackled than mathematics which is 'abstract'.)

As an example of a simple investigation with a dice game, *Lu-Lu* (Section 6.1) led to a class investigation into the number of different totals which could be scored in two throws of the stones. Young, low-ability pupils were able to produce the following:

Total score	Possible throws	
0	0	0
1	1	0
2	2	0
	1	1
3	3	0
	2	1
4	4	0
	3	1
	2	2

and so on . . . which leads to a total of

$$1 + 1 + 2 + 2 + 3 + 3 + 4 + 4 + 5 + 5 + 6 +$$
$$5 + 5 + 4 + 4 + 3 + 3 + 2 + 2 + 1 + 1 = 66$$

possible outcomes for two throws of the stones and the generation of some simple patterns.

A Korean porcelain figure of a clown and giant dice from the Korean pavilion at Expo '86 in Vancouver.

7.6 Presentation of work to pupils

The following are examples of some of the 'worksheets' given to different groups of children:

Pong Hau K'i

This is a game from China which is played by two people on a board like that shown below:

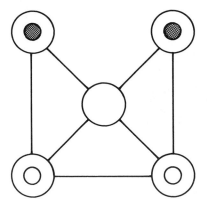

Figure 7.7

Each player has two stones of different colours (black and white) which are placed as shown at the start. Players move alternately and, at a turn, move one stone to an adjacent empty point. The aim is to block the opponent's stones.

- -

Investigate the game

Some questions you may wish to consider:

1. Is it better to be black or white?
2. Is it better to go first or second?
3. How many possible positions are there?
4. Can a win be forced? If so, how?

When you have completed your investigation of this game, invent a similar one of your own.

Tchuka Ruma

This is an East Indian game for one player. It is played on a board which has 5 holes with 2 pebbles in each hole at the start – except the Ruma which is empty.

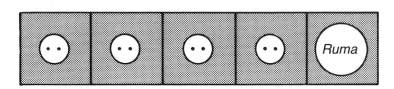

Figure 7.8

You must lift the pebbles from any hole and 'sow' them from left to right, dropping one in each hole as you pass. For example, suppose you selected the extreme left-hand hole to begin with:

```
        Start:  2  2  2  2  0
   After move:  0  3  3  2  0
```

You now lift the pebbles from the hole in which you finished and 'sow' these again from left to right.

If the last pebble sown falls in an empty hole you lose. If not, you sow again starting from the hole in which you finished. If the sowing ends in the Ruma you may select any hole to begin the next move.

If the Ruma is reached with more than one piece in hand, you continue at the extreme left-hand hole.

The aim is to get all the pebbles in the Ruma.

- -

Investigate the game. Can it be done?

Some questions you may wish to consider:

1. What would be good positions to arrive at?
2. What happens if the number of pieces per hole is changed?
3. What happens if the number of holes is changed?

Tabula

This is a game something like Backgammon. It was played by the Romans in the first century AD. Two players each have 15 pieces to race round a board.

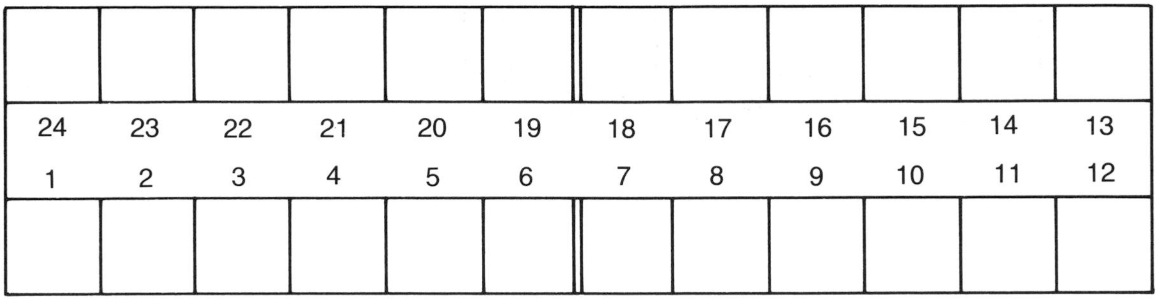

24	23	22	21	20	19	18	17	16	15	14	13
1	2	3	4	5	6	7	8	9	10	11	12

Figure 7.9

Players take turns to throw three dice and all pieces enter the board at the same place and move in the same direction. When a player has thrown they can decide whether to move one, two or three pieces. For example, if 3, 4, 5 is thrown then:

- one piece can be moved by 12, or
- two pieces can be moved 7 and 5, or 8 and 4, or 3 and 9, or
- three pieces can be moved 3, 4 and 5.

---

1. How many different throws are possible with (i) two dice and (ii) with three dice?
2. How many opening moves are possible in Tabula after a player's first throw with (i) two dice and (ii) three dice?
3. Invent some rules of your own for a game based on this board and 15 pieces for each player.

Seega

This is a game played by young Egyptians. The board is as below – one player has pieces marked 'X', the other pieces marked 'O'.

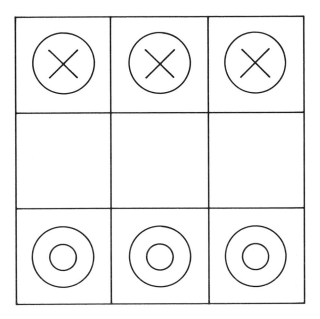

Figure *7.10*

Players play alternately and, on each turn, can move a piece 1 or 2 squares *in any direction* (including diagonal) but must not pass over another piece.

The first player to get three pieces in a straight line (diagonal included) *other than along the original starting line* is the winner.

- -

1. Play some games. Who wins? Does the starting player have an advantage?
2. Find a way to write down the moves for a game and record the moves for a game which is played.
3. How many opening moves are possible?
4. How many positions are possible after each player has made one move?

7.7 Games and mathematics in a broader context

Undoubtedly most games are fun to play. Any mathematics arising from a game is a bonus for the teacher. It would be foolish to ignore other gains which might be made from the use of games with children.

Apart from any investigation which might arise from a game, there is the act of *recording* results and maybe organising competitions between pupils – how many games do we need to play in a class knock-out tournament? How do we decide on choice of opponents and order of play? Many organisational skills can be developed.

There are links with many other subjects which can be explored. Consider, for example, the number of different countries mentioned in the brief descriptions of games in this book, or the references to different periods of history – there is scope here to involve other traditional 'subjects'. The game *Tablut* might lead to consideration of the work of Linnaeus and thence to work on classification in biology. A comparison of Victorian and contemporary board games might produce some profitable discussion.

It is almost impossible to ignore the *practical* possibilities which exist. Games can nearly always be made with the most basic and easily obtainable materials. Making boards and pieces for the games described might involve woodwork and artistic decoration or, at a simpler level, paper, card, glue, scissors and a few coloured pencils will suffice for the production of playing equipment. Great ingenuity and originality are possible in providing pieces for games where original rules are not clear and where the exact nature of equipment used is not known. If games are actually *made*, a whole collection for the use of a particular group of children can soon be built up.

7.8 Assessment of investigational work

The 'threat' of assessment can easily inhibit pupils when engaged in investigational activity. However, many teachers will be faced with situations in which they *have* to carry out some kind of evaluation of work. Most assessment has to be based largely on written work but other methods – e.g. oral response, tape recordings, computer programs etc. – might also be used. The following check-list (based broadly on one given in Garrard (1986)) might prove useful in assessing work arising from some of the games in this book:

   (i) pupil's approach, attitude and interest,
  (ii) development from initial problem,
 (iii) creativity and originality,
 (iv) recording and writing up of work done,
  (v) ability to communicate findings to others,
 (vi) mathematical and logical insight,
(vii) possible extensions and/or variations.

It is not easy to get pupils to produce good, coherent accounts of work done (as some of the examples earlier in this chapter illustrate) but most teachers are likely to have in mind a list of points, similar to those above, which need to be taken into consideration in any assessment.

8. Comments on suggested investigations

Chapter 2: Games of position

Noughts and Crosses

 (i) There are *three* possible opening moves (centre, corner and middle of a side).
 (ii) After each player has made one move there are *twelve* positions possible and from *seven* of these the first player should win.
(iii) If the road numbers in *Jam* are written in a magic square e.g.

$$8 \quad 1 \quad 6$$
$$3 \quad 5 \quad 7$$
$$4 \quad 9 \quad 2$$

then rows, columns and diagonals represent intersections of roads (e.g. 8, 1, 6 represents the point where the roads with these numbers meet) and capturing these roads through a town is the same as getting a line in *Noughts and Crosses*.
(iv) If two players play with counters marked 1 to 9, scoring a total of 15 is the same as securing a line in *Noughts and Crosses*. The game will not be won unless a player makes a mistake but slight modification of the rules can lead to some interesting alternative games.

Three Men's Morris

 (i) The initial part of the game is the same as *Noughts and Crosses*. The centre point is always a good one to control.
 (ii) If reflections and rotations of the board are not considered the same, there are 1680 possible positions with all six men on the board.

Achi

(i) The first player should always win. Suppose the first
player place a ● in the centre.
  (*a*) If the second player places ○ in a corner, moves
  can proceed as in Figure 8.1,

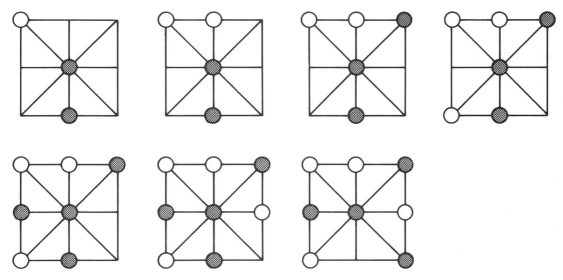

Figure *8.1*

and the first player (●) wins in two more
moves.

(*b*) If the second player places ○ in the middle of a
side, play as in Figure 8.2

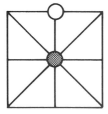 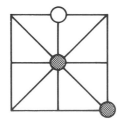 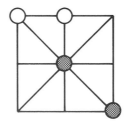 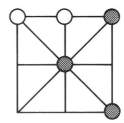

Figure *8.2*

gives the first player a win.

Six Men's Morris

(ii) 36 positions are possible after one move each (after
allowing for rotations and reflections of the board).

(iii) It is possible to have twelve pieces on the board
without a row being formed.

Nine and Twelve Men's Morris

(ii) On the first board, the length is 28 cm and on the second $28 + 4\sqrt{2}$ cm.

(iii) A spider would walk 31 cm and $31.5 + 7\sqrt{2}$ cm (= 41.398 cm).

'Modern' Seega

(i) There are seven possible opening moves.

(ii) After one move by each player, 38 positions are possible.

(In both cases reflections are not counted as the same.)

Traditional Seega

Since B must imitate A, it is only necessary to find the number of ways in which A can place two pieces on the board.

Mulinello Quadrupio

(i) There are 35 squares and 96 triangles.

Pong Hau K'i

(i) There are 30 positions if reflections are allowed.

(iii) Either player can always force a draw. Defeat only occurs if one player allows both pieces to be trapped on one side.

Mu Torere

(i) A draw can always be achieved. There is a possible trap as shown in Figure 8.3.

In Figure 8.3a, white has to move with a choice of 1–8 or 7–8. The latter is fatal since black will answer 6–7. The 'V' shape of black's pieces at 5, 6 and P should not be allowed to split open.

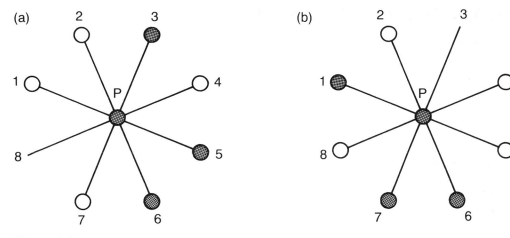

Figure 8.3

In Figure 8.3b, white has a choice of 2–3 or 4–3. The former will be followed by 1–2, 8–1, 7–8, opening the 'V' and winning the game for black.

There is an unpreventable circular movement around the edge of the board – possession of the putahi is essential to winning.

Pentalpha

If the points are labelled as in Figure 8.4 a solution is as follows:

652, 076, 478, 980, 359, 763, 187, 591, 564.

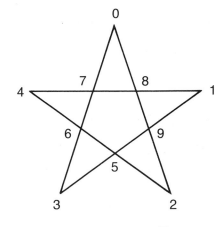

Figure 8.4

English Solitaire

If the notation of Figure 2.19 is used, the game can be solved as follows:

1 D2–D4 **2** F3–D3 **3** E1–E3 **4** E4–E2 **5** C1–E1
6 E1–E3 **7** E6–E4 **8** G5–E5 **9** D5–F5 **10** G3–G5
11 G5–E5 **12** B5–D5 **13** C7–C5 **14** C4–C6 **15** E7–C7
16 C7–C5 **17** C2–C4 **18** A3–C3 **19** D3–B3
20 A5–A3 **21** A3–C3 **22** D5–D3 **23** D3–B3
24 B3–B5 **25** B5–D5 **26** D5–F5 **27** F4–D4 **28** C4–E4
29 E3–E5 **30** F5–D5 **31** D6–D4

French Solitaire

The following solutions use the notation of Figure 2.20.

The Cross of St Andrew: D2–D4, F2–D2, D1–D3, B2–D2, C4–C2, E4–E2, C1–C3, E1–E3, A4–C4, G4–E4, B6–B4, F6–F4, D5–B5, D3–D5, D5–F5, F4–D4, C4–C2, C2–E2, E2–E4, E4–C4, B4–D4, A5–C5, D7–D5, D5–B5, C7–C5, B5–D5, G5–E5, E5–C5, A3–C3, G3–E3, E7–E5.

The Professor and His Students: D2–D4, B2–D2, C4–C2, D2–B2, A3–C3, B5–B3, C3–A3, D5–B5, C7–C5, B5–D5, E6–C6, E5–C5, C5–C7, G5–E5, F3–F5, E5–G5, D4–F4, E2–E4, F4–D4.

Chapter 3:   Mancala games

Mancala II

(i) Start with: 2 2 2 2 2 2

    A leaves: 0 3 3 2 2 2

and then B leaves: 004332, 030333, 033033, 133203 or 143220 and A wins only if B leaves the last of these. Otherwise B wins on their next move.

(ii) Start with: 3 3 3 3 3 3

    A leaves: 0 4 4 4 3 3

and then B leaves: 005544, 140544, 154044, 154404 or 155430 and if B leaves the first of these they win on their next move.

(iii) Start with: 4 4 4 4 4 4

and if A plays without errors, they can ensure a win on their third move.

Mankal'ah L'ib Al-Ghashim

(i) If the board is kept as it is, you will win.
(ii) 35 arrangements are possible. (The problem is to place 4 objects in 4 holes.) Thus an opponent can

present you with 35 different positions – which
would you accept? In particular, what about
symmetrical arrangements such as:

        2 4   or   4 2
        4 2   2 4?

Any game is 'won' as soon as the board is set up!

(iii) The problem is that of placing 24 objects in 12
holes. This can be done in $^{35}C_{11}$ ways (i.e.
417 225 900) (see also analysis of *Nyout* in Section
7.4). Thus there are over four hundred million
possible games!

Gabata

(i) Since the board is symmetrical players reach:

            Player Y
        4   4   0 $\underline{5}$ 5   1
        4   0   4   4   0   4
        1   5 $\underline{5}$ 0   4   4
            Player X

with the players in the underlined positions. Both
land in an empty hole on the next move – suggest a
way of resolving the situation!

(ii) The position:

        5   5   1   0   5   1
        5   $\underline{5}$ 3   4   0   4
        0   4   4   0   4   4

is reached with both players at the same
hole – whoever picks up the faster gets to an
empty hole!

(iii) The position must have arisen from X and Y
sowing, landing in empty holes at the same time and
then X beating Y to the move into another empty
hole.

(iv) One obvious position from which X can capture 17
pieces would be:

        0   17
        0   0
        0   1   !

Kiriabu

(i) The player who starts should win.

(ii) Since clockwise and anticlockwise moves are
possible either player could achieve at least a draw!

Ize-Ozin-Egbe

(ii)

```
1  1  1
1  1  1
```

takes 34 moves before repeating.

```
2  2  2
2  2  2
```

takes 747 moves.

```
1  2  1
1  2  1
```

takes 19, 84, 72 moves starting with 1, 2, 1
respectively.

```
1  3  1
1  3  1
```

takes 72, 31, 849 moves starting with 1, 3, 1
respectively.

Tchuka Ruma

(i) The only possible solution is:

```
2  2  2  2  0;   2  2  0  3  1;   3  3  0  0  2;
3  0  1  1  3;   3  0  0  2  3;
4  0  0  0  4;   0  1  1  1  5;
0  1  1  0  6;   0  0  2  0  6;
0  0  0  1  7;   0  0  0  0  8;   i.e. 10 moves.
```

(ii) There is no solution with 6 holes, a Ruma and 3
pieces per hole. A solution *can* be found with 8
holes, a Ruma and 4 pieces per hole. A large
number of possibilities exist!

(iii) In a circular arrangement of cups, with 3 cups
containing 1 piece each, the game is possible. Also
with 4 cups and 2 pieces each (as in *Tchuka Ruma*).
It cannot be done with 3 cups and 2 or 3 pieces nor
with 4 cups and 1, 3 or 4 pieces.

Some other possible 'solitaire' investigations

The following pattern emerges:

Number of single seeds	Number of moves
3	3
4	4
5	6
6	9
7	10
8	12
9	13
10	17
11	18
12	20
13	21
14	23
15	25
16	26

and some further analysis could be carried out. For example, if all seeds move only 1 place at a time then n seeds require $\frac{1}{2}n(n-1)$ moves. But every time a 2 is sown, 2 of these moves are saved, a 3 lifted saves 5 moves, a 4 lifted saves 9 moves . . . So, for example, with 11 seeds, 55 single moves are needed but the best sowing uses 1 four, 4 threes and 4 twos giving a number of moves:

$$55 - (1 \times 9) - (4 \times 5) - (4 \times 2) = 18.$$

Chapter 4: War games

Shaturanga

Assume that a Ship 'attacks' *two* squares in each diagonal direction.
  (i) 24 Ships can be placed so that no two are attacking each other. One way is shown in Figure 8.5a. – several other arrangements are possible.
  (ii) 12 Ships can attack all squares between them (see Figure 8.5b, for example).

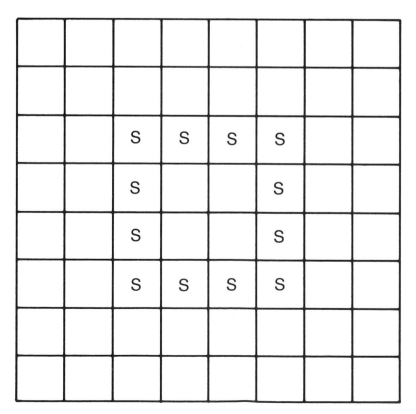

Figure 8.5a

Figure 8.5b

Lau Kati Kata

(i) There are only four positions possible after two moves by each player (if reflections of the board are considered the same).

(ii) With one black piece left to oppose two white pieces, black should be able to force a draw – but a mistake could leave black trapped.

The Maharajah and the Sepoys

(i) On the board at the start, the Maharajah commands the following numbers of squares from each position:

```
19  21  23  23  23  23  21  19
19  23  26  27  27  26  23  19
21  25  29  30  30  29  25  21
21  25  29  30  30  29  25  21
19  23  26  27  27  26  23  19
19  21  23  23  23  23  21  19

 .   .   .   .   .   .   .   .
 .   .   .   .   .   .   .   .
```

This suggests that one of the middle '30' squares might be a good starting position.

(ii) On a board with no other pieces the numbers of squares commanded by the Maharajah are:

```
23  24  25  25  25  25  24  23
23  27  29  29  29  29  27  23
25  29  33  33  33  33  29  25
25  29  33  35  35  33  29  25
25  29  33  35  35  33  29  25
25  29  33  33  33  33  29  25
23  27  29  29  29  29  27  25
23  24  25  25  25  25  24  23
```

Tablut

(i) There are 10 opening moves for the Muscovites and seven for the Swedes.

(ii) The Swedes can win in a minimum of three moves and the Muscovites in a minimum of four.

(iii) The game appears to be delicately balanced and any changes in the forces seem to make the game one-sided, usually in favour of the Swedes.

113

Fox and Geese

(i) The fox cannot be trapped with fewer than four geese.

(ii) The 'best' opening move for the geese is probably to move the piece on the extreme right (or left).

(iii) There are seven ways of placing a single fox, 160 ways of placing one fox and one goose.

(iv) If reflections and rotations of the board are not taken into account, there are 29 904 336 positions possible with the fox and six geese.

Lambs and Tigers

(i) A single tiger can be placed in 12 ways.

(ii) With all the pieces on the board, if reflections are not regarded as being the same, there are 27 457 584 positions.

(iii) At least six lambs are needed to trap all the tigers.

Cows and Leopards

(ii) A win cannot be forced without at least four cows. (The leopards can be trapped at the outer corners of the four triangles.)

Vultures and Crows

(i) The vulture must kill at least four crows.

(ii) There are only 10 positions possible with one crow and one vulture on the board.

Chapter 5: Race games

Tau

(i) The following 'pattern' emerges if smaller boards are considered:

3 squares can be arranged in 1 symmetrical board
4 squares can be arranged in 3 symmetrical boards
5 squares can be arranged in 5 symmetrical boards
6 squares can be arranged in 8 symmetrical boards
7 squares can be arranged in 12 symmetrical boards
8 squares can be arranged in 26 symmetrical boards
9 squares can be arranged in ? symmetrical boards

Senat

(i) If both players keep throwing even numbers, all pieces reach 'safe' squares without capture. A total of 110 throws (55 for each player) is needed to complete the game – these throws involve 95 × '4', 5 × '3', 5 × '2' and 5 × '1'.

(ii) After two moves there are 519 possible positions and, in general, with n pieces for each player, ($n > 2$) there are

$$4n^2 + 12n - 1$$

positions possible after 2 moves (see also Chapter 7).

Tabula

(i) Two dice can be thrown in 21 ways and three dice in 56 ways.

(ii) There are 32 possible moves with two dice, 128 with three dice.

(iii) The 'best' throw for Zeno might have been 4, 3, 3, for example.

(iv) Eight throws are needed to finish a game with 8 pieces on a twelve square board.

(v) 25 throws are needed for a full board with 15 pieces.

Chasing the girls

(i) With six pieces of each colour on the board there are 2 498 640 144 possible positions ($^{24}C_6 \times {}^{18}C_6$) – no 'doubling up' is allowed.

(ii) For a 12 point board and 3 pieces each there are 18 480 positions.

Nyout

(i) The quickest possible game has six moves (throw five '5's' and then anything).

(ii) Lengths of possible routes for each piece are 11, 16, 20, 21. Thus to get four pieces home, four of these numbers are needed. There are 35 ways of selecting the four numbers (see also Chapter 7).

(iv) With 4, 5, 4, 5, 4, 2 a player could get two pieces home and move two others 4 spaces.

Ka-wa-su-suts

(i) 0, 2, 3, 5, 10, 12, 13, 15 are possible scores.

(ii) The sequences required must all add up to 12, thus (excluding '0's) the following are possible:

6×2, $\quad 4 \times 3$, $\quad 1 \times 12$, $\quad 10 + 2$, $\quad 5 + 5 + 2$,
$5 + 3 + 2 + 2$, $\quad 3 + 3 + 2 + 2 + 2$.

Pachisi

(i) The smallest number of throws needed is 8 (e.g. $6 \times 25 + 1 \times 6 + 1 \times 3$).

(ii) (*a*) If every throw was a 10, then 22 throws would be needed. With throws of 10, a piece must get to the square 10 from home and then throw a 10. The square required is 74 from the start and there are 68 squares on the 'outer' circuit so we need:

$$(74 + 68j) = 10k$$

(where j = no. of complete laps done and k = no. of throws). The first solution occurs when $j = 2$ and $k = 21$ and so 22 throws are needed.

(*b*) If every throw was a 25, then 36 throws would be needed.

With throws of 25 a piece must get to the square 25 spaces from home and then throw 25. The requisite square is 59 from the start and, since there are 68 squares on the 'outer' circuit, this square is reached after k throws of 25 and j complete laps where:

$$(59 + 68j) = 25k$$

The first solution of this equation occurs when $j = 12$ and $k = 35$. Hence 36 throws are needed.

Chapter 6:   Dice, calculation and other games

Pitch and Toss

(i) The probability that the game finishes before the third player gets a throw is $^{27}/_{64}$.
(Possible outcomes are:

Player 1, 3 correct: Probability $^1/_8$.
Player 1, 2 correct, Player 2, 1 correct: Probability $^3/_{16}$.
Player 1, 1 correct, Player 2, 2 correct: Probability $^3/_{32}$.
Player 1, 0 correct, Player 2, 3 correct: Probability $^1/_{64}$.)

(ii) The probability that the third player has three pennies to throw is $^1/_{64}$.
(iii) There are ten possible outcomes after the first two players have thrown.

Dittar Pradesh

The probability that the pool is won is 0.534.

Lu-Lu

(i) Possible scores are all numbers from 0 to 20 and there are 66 ways in which the stones can fall. (See also Section 7.5.)
(ii) A score of 50 can be reached in exactly 6 throws in 35 ways.
(iii) As an example of a problem from a smaller game, with 3 stones (marked 1, 2, 3) 20 can be scored in 5 throws in 23 ways.

Ave Victrix

(i) There are 20 possible scores in a single turn:

4 (retires), 9, 11, 12, 13, 14 (wins), 15, 16, 17, 19, 20, 23, 25, 28, 29, 31, 32, 68, 84, 116.

(ii) One way to score exactly 1000 in 10 throws would be to throw four princes and four eagles five times each.

Four–Five–Six

(i) There is a probability of $^{27}/_{216}$ that the banker wins outright and of $^{21}/_{216}$ that he loses outright.

Poker Dice

(i) There are 252 possible initial throws.
(ii) If K, K are rethrown, then the player must get at least one J. The probability of this is $^{11}/_{36}$. If J, J, J are rethrown, the player must get at least two kings and the probability is $^{16}/_{216}$.

Rithmomachia

(i) Both ends of the board have the pattern:

$$
\begin{array}{llllll}
 & & n & m & p & q \\
(n+1)^2 & (m+1)^2 & n^2 & m^2 & p^2 & q^2 \ldots \\
(n+1)(2n+1) & (m+1)(2m+1) & n^2+n & m^2+m & \ldots \\
(2n+1)^2 & (2m+1)^2 & \ldots
\end{array}
$$

where $m = n + 2$, $p = n + 4$, and $q = n + 6$.

(iii) Much work can be done on sets of four numbers which contain two or more of the three progressions. In general, sets of numbers of the forms $(4k, 6k, 9k, 12k)$ and $(3k, 4k, 6k, 9k)$ will contain triples in each of the three types of progression. Thus there are three sets of numbers on the board – (3, 4, 6, 9); (4, 6, 9, 12); (15, 20, 30, 45) – which form all three types of progression. In addition the board contains 60 sets of numbers in AP *and* GP; 41 in AP *and* HP; 15 in GP *and* HP.

Examples include:

AP and GP: (2, 9, 12, 16); (49, 91, 169, 289);
              (81, 153, 225, 289)
AP and HP: (2, 9, 16, 72); (72, 81, 90, 120)
GP and HP: (3, 5, 15, 45); (9, 15, 45, 225);
              (25, 45, 81, 225)

Pegs in Holes

If 123456 represents the position with a peg in hole 1 in
column 1, hole 2 in column 2 etc. then a solution to the
problem is 246135.

With similar notation, solutions are possible as follows:

4×4 board: 2413
5×5 board: 24135.
7×7 board: 2461357
8×8 board: 24683175.

(The 8×8 problem is the well-known one of placing 8
queens on a chessboard.)

Officers and Nationalities

The problem is insoluble for a 6×6 array.

With 100 soldiers the problem can be done. If we use
the numbers 0 to 9 to represent the ranks and the
nationalities (so that e.g. 03 represents the lowest rank
and the fourth nationality) a solution is as below:

46	57	68	70	81	02	13	24	35	99
71	94	37	65	12	40	29	06	88	53
93	26	54	01	38	19	85	77	60	42
15	43	80	27	09	74	66	58	92	31
32	78	16	89	63	55	47	91	04	20
67	05	79	52	44	36	90	83	21	18
84	69	41	33	25	98	72	10	56	07
59	30	22	14	97	61	08	45	73	86
28	11	03	96	50	87	34	62	49	75
00	82	95	48	76	23	51	39	17	64

This solution is taken from Ball and Coxeter (1974) –
the reader is referred to this book for more detailed
discussion of both this problem and the one which
follows.

Kirkman's Schoolgirls

A solution is:

Day 1: 1, 6, 11; 2, 7, 12; 3, 8, 13; 4, 9, 14; 5, 10, 15.
Day 2: 1, 2, 5; 3, 4, 6; 8, 9, 12; 10, 11, 14; 13, 15, 6.
Day 3: 2, 3, 6; 4, 5, 8; 9, 10, 13; 11, 12, 15; 14, 1, 7.
Day 4: 5, 6, 9; 7, 8, 11; 12, 13, 1; 14, 15, 3; 2, 4, 10.
Day 5: 3, 5, 11; 4, 6, 12; 7, 9, 15; 8, 10, 1; 13, 14, 2.
Day 6: 5, 7, 13; 6, 8, 14; 9, 11, 2; 10, 12, 3; 15, 1, 4.
Day 7: 11, 13, 4; 12, 14, 5; 15, 2, 8; 1, 3, 9; 6, 7, 10.

Noro

A player could win in 14 moves.

Marvellous '26'

(i) There are 33 ways of making 26 from the twelve numbers using 4 at a time. There are 7 ways using 6 at a time.

(ii) One way of obtaining 26 on each side of both triangles *and* around the central hexagon is:

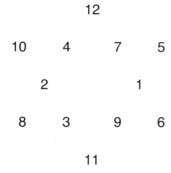

The puzzle lends itself to much useful number work and pattern spotting.

References and further reading

Addison, Stephen (1983) *100 Other Games to Play on a Chessboard*, Peter Owen

Ainslie, Tom (1975) *Ainslie's Complete Hoyle*, New English Library

Arnold, P. (1985) *The Book of Games*, W. H. Smith

Averbach, B. and Chein, D. (1980) *Mathematics: Problem Solving Through Recreational Mathematics*, Freeman

Ball, W. W. and Coxeter, H. S. M. (1974) *Mathematical Recreations and Essays*, University of Toronto Press

Beasley, J. D. (1985) *The Ins and Outs of Peg Solitaire*, Oxford University Press

Bell, R. C. (1969) *Board and Table Games from Many Civilisations*, Oxford University Press

Bell, R. C. (1973) *Discovering Old Board Games*, Shire Publications

Bell, R. C. (1983) *The Boardgame Book*, Marshall Cavendish

Berlekamp, E. R., Conway, J. H. and Guy, R. K. (1982) *Winning Ways for Your Mathematical Plays*, Academic Press

Bishop, D. (1987) 'African pastime sows the seeds of skill and chance', in *The Micro User*, Vol 4 No 11

Brandreth, Giles (1981) *Everyman's Indoor Games*, J. M. Dent and Sons

Brill, R. L. (1985) 'A project for the low-budget mathematics laboratory: the game of kalah', in *Games and Puzzles for Elementary and Middle School Mathematics*, National Council of Teachers of Mathematics

Cartwright, M. (1986) 'Crackly phones and the schoolgirl problem', *New Scientist*, 3 July 1986

Cassell (1973) *Cassell's Book of Indoor Amusements, Card Games and Fireside Fun*, Cassell and Co.

Cockcroft Report (1982) *Mathematics Counts*, HMSO, London

Degrazia, J. (1949) *Maths is Fun*, Allen and Unwin

Dunford, J. (1982) in *Teaching Mathematics* (ed. Michael Cornelius), Croom Helm

Egharevba, J. U. (1949) *Benin Games*, Benin

Emery, W. B. (1961) *Archaic Egypt*, Penguin Books

Evans, R. (1976) 'Pong Hau K'i', in *Games and Puzzles*, No. 53

Falkener, E. (1961) *Games Ancient and Oriental and How to Play Them*, Dover

Garrard, W. (1986) *I Don't Know: Let's Find Out*, Suffolk County Council

Gelli, J. (1900) *Come Posso Divertirmi?*, Milan

Grunfeld, F. W. (1975) *Games of the World*, Holt, Rinehart and Winston

Haggerty, J. B. (1985) 'Kalah – an ancient game of mathematical skill' in *Games and Puzzles for Elementary and Middle School Mathematics*, National Council of Teachers of Mathematics

King, C. E. (1978) *The Encyclopedia of Toys*, Robert Hale

Lane, E. W. (1890) *An account of the manners and customs of modern Egyptians*, Ward Lock and Co.

Linnaeus, C. (1811) *Lachesis Lapponica*, London

Love, B. (1979) *Great Board Games*, Edbury Press and Michael Joseph

McConville, R. (1974) *The History of Board Games*, Creative Publications Inc.

Millington, R. (1979) *Games and Puzzles for Addicts*, M. & J. Hobbs in association with Michael Joseph

Murray, H. J. R. (1978) *A History of Board Games Other than Chess*, Hacker Art Books Inc.

Open University (1978) *Mathematics Foundation Course*

Pankhurst, R. (1971) Gabata and Related Board-Games of Ethiopia and the Horn of Africa' in *Ethiopia Observer*, vol. XIV, pp. 154–206

Pennycook, A. (1973) *The Indoor Games Book*, Faber and Faber

Polya, G. (1957) *How to Solve It*, Doubleday Anchor Books

Ruderman, H. D. (1985) 'Nu Tic-Tac-Toe' in *Games and Puzzles for Elementary and Middle School Mathematics*, National Council of Teachers of Mathematics

Sackson, S. (1969) *A Gamut of Games*, Random House

Schuh, F. (1968) *The Master Book of Mathematical Recreations*, Dover

Sheppard, R. and Wilkinson, J. (1986) *Fifty Board Games*, Suffolk Education Authority

Waddington (1984) *Waddington's Illustrated Encyclopaedia of Games*, Pan Books

White, G. (1971) *Antique Toys and their Background*, Chancellor Press

Whitehouse, F. R. B. (1971) *Table Games of Georgian and Victorian Days*, Priory Press

• Index

Names of games are given in italics